W9-BGA-559

The Holocaust Remembered Series

The Holocaust Overview

Ann Byers

Enslow Publishers, Inc.
40 Industrial Road   PO Box 38
Box 398   Aldershot
Berkeley Heights, NJ 07922   Hants GU12 6BP
USA   UK
http://www.enslow.com

Library of Congress Cataloging-Publication Data

Byers, Ann.
    The Holocaust overview / Ann Byers.
        p. cm. — (The Holocaust remembered series)
    Includes bibliographical references.
    Summary: Examines Hitler's treatment of the Jews, before and during
World War II, from their early exclusion from German society to the later
policy of extermination.
    ISBN 0-7660-1062-7
    1. Holocaust, Jewish (1939–1945)—Juvenile literature. 2. Germany—
Politics and government—1933–1945—Juvenile literature. [1. Germany—
Politics and government—1933–1945.] I. Title. II. Series.
    D804.34.B94   1998
    940.53'18—dc21   97-37637
                                                      CIP
                                                         AC

Printed in the United States of America

10 9 8 7 6 5 4 3

Illustration Credits: AP/Wide World Photos, 39; Bundesarchiv, courtesy of
USHMM Photo Archives, 31; Documentationsarchiv des Osterreichischen
Widerstandes, courtesy of USHMM Photo Archives, 29; Created by Enslow
Publishers, Inc., 80, 103; Richard Freimark, courtesy of USHMM Photo
Archives, 9, 23, 26; KZ Gedenkstatte Dachau, courtesy of USHMM Photo
Archives, 56, 62; Library of Congress, courtesy of USHMM Photo Archives, 60;
Main Commission for the Investigation of Nazi War Crimes, courtesy of
USHMM Photo Archives, 53, 69, 86; William O. McWorkman, courtesy of
USHMM Photo Archives, 16, 105; National Archives, courtesy of USHMM
Photo Archives, 6, 47, 77, 97, 108; National Museum in Majdanek, courtesy of
USHMM Photo Archives, 89; *The New York Times*, courtesy of USHMM Photo
Archives, 43; Leopold Page Photographic Collection, courtesy of USHMM Photo
Archives, 71; Rijksinstituut voor Oorlogsdocumentatie, courtesy of USHMM
Photo Archives, 66; Dr. Alfred B. Sundquist, courtesy of USHMM Photo
Archives, 100; Courtesy of USHMM Photo Archives, 12, 19, 29, 33, 34, 41, 45,
51; USHMM, courtesy of Yad Vashem, 47; Yad Vashem Photo Archives, courtesy ·
of USHMM Photo Archives, 93, 94; YIVO Institute for Jewish Research,
courtesy of USHMM Photo Archives, 7.

Cover Illustration: National Archives.

Contents

Introduction:

Anti-Semitism

The sign at the entrance to the city was clear: *Jews Strictly Forbidden in This Town*. If that warning failed, then the notices above the shops were unmistakable: *Jews Not Admitted*. At the bakery, the butcher shop, the dairy, even the pharmacy, money from Jews was not welcome. Outside the city, at a dangerous bend in the road, a caution was posted: *Drive Carefully! Sharp Curve! Jews 75 Miles an Hour*. The year was 1936. The place was Germany.[1]

Anti-Semitism—intense dislike for and deliberate persecution of Jews—can be traced back in history to ancient times, starting with the differences in beliefs between Judaism and Christianity. Over the following centuries, negative stereotypes of the Jews took form and were spread throughout Europe. However, the Jews managed to flourish, a people without a country, sharing only their faith and beliefs.

In the early 1900s, anti-Semitism took on a new form that falsely accused the Jews of being the carriers

Anger and protest over the Versailles Treaty caused many to focus their blame on the Jews. This demonstration in Vienna, Austria, shortly after World War I, echoed German anti-Semitism. The banner reads "Away with the Jewish press: lies, corruption, rubbish."

of sickness, economic crisis, poverty, and political conflicts; in other words, all the ills that afflicted mankind. This sentiment spread, especially in some parts of France and Germany, from scholars down to common people.

After World War I (1914–1918), Germany, which started then lost the war, was rocked by economic depression, political uncertainty, and social unrest. As the German people looked for ways to vent their frustrations, the Jews seemed a ready-made target—in spite of their many contributions to Germany in the

These German soldiers display their anti-Semitism by tormenting and pulling on the beards of these elderly Jewish men. The Jewish man on the right is Shachna Rubinstein. He was killed at the Treblinka extermination camp in 1942 or 1943.

arts, the sciences, and the humanities. Nonetheless, many people were ready to believe that all the misery that plagued their nation was the doing of this one group. By the end of the 1920s, anti-Semitism had become a way of life for some Germans.

When Adolf Hitler led the Nazi party to gain control of Germany in 1933, he made discrimination against Jews national policy. Hitler's fanatical anti-Semitism, his insatiable appetite for power, and his ruthless ability to manipulate and control his followers spelled disaster for the Jews. Before he was even firmly in position as Germany's leader, his writings and speeches contained the dark seeds for what would become a program of genocide—murder of an entire group of people.

The storm that would ravage the entire continent had four phases. Spawned in a climate of hate, it began with the black cloud of persecution. Before Hitler took office, Jews were unjustly slandered in vicious newspaper articles, made fun of in cruel pamphlets and posters, and denounced in mean-spirited speeches. Harassment of Jews and crimes against them went unpunished. This first stage could be called exclusion, because Jews were stripped of their possessions, their rights, and their citizenship. They were excluded from public office, from most professions, and from many businesses. Politicians and government officials instigated riots, boycotts, and fires and blamed them on Jews.

After exclusion came expulsion. Jews were first bullied and then forced to leave the country. Thousands fled the oppressive tyranny, and thousands more were deported involuntarily.

Then, in the middle of this expulsion, Hitler plunged all of Europe into a war that eventually encompassed much of the world. His goals in starting a war were bigger than his passion against the Jews. He wanted "living space" for the German people, he wanted to expand the borders of Germany, and he wanted to rule over all of Europe. But the war would also provide, he thought, the justification, the camouflage, and the machinery to rid Europe of Jews forever.

World War II began on September 1, 1939, with Germany's surprise invasion of Poland. The new land gave Hitler space to put the Jews he was expelling from Germany. Three million Jews already lived in Poland at the start of World War II.

Adolf Hitler was the mastermind of the Holocaust and, with Heinrich Himmler (to Hitler's right), Rudolf Hess (to Himmler's right), and the other Nazi officials, led the German people towards the Final Solution. Himmler was the head of the German police, including the feared Gestapo and Schutzstaffel (SS). Hess served as deputy leader of the Nazi Party and was Hitler's private secretary.

The next step in his program was enclosure. All the Jews living in the conquered territories were closed off by themselves, concentrated in crowded parts of cities called ghettos. They were forced to wear yellow stars on their clothing to mark them as undesirables. Then walls or fences were built around the ghettos, sentries were posted, and residents were forbidden to leave or to have any contact with people outside.

After conquering Poland, Hitler invaded other nations and more Jews came under his rule. They, too, were separated from their countrymen and sent to concentration camps in Poland and Germany. These camps, originally intended for political opponents of the Nazis, were also used to house prisoners of war and the archenemies of the state: Jewish men, women, and children. Even in the camps, the Jews' yellow badges set them apart from the other internees who included criminals, gypsies, homosexuals, and other asocials who the Nazis considered to be outside the German mainstream.

When Hitler tried to stretch his dominion over the Soviet Union, his war in Europe bogged down and his war against the Jews heated up. At that point he implemented the last step in his anti-Semitic program: extermination. Each preceding stage had brought death to thousands. During the exclusion phase, police and citizens in hundreds of cities had taken the property of their Jewish neighbors, and had killed many. In the expulsion stage, Jews perished on long journeys in overcrowded railroad cars. In the ghettos and camps of the enclosure phase, thousands died every day from insufficient food and excessive brutality. Hitler's final solution to what he called the Jewish Problem, however, was the deliberate murder of every Jew by any means: indiscriminate killing, starvation, overwork, savage cruelty, systematic execution.

This four-stage program—with death at every step—has come to be known as the Holocaust, which means "sacrifice completely consumed by fire." In only twelve years, two thirds of the Jews of Europe perished, their bodies buried or burned in the fires of hundreds of crematoriums.

They were murdered to appease the maniacal hatred of a man who saw himself as a "Lord of the Earth."

Climate of Hate

G ermany, like much of Europe, had a long history of religious intolerance against Jews. By the time Adolf Hitler came to power in 1933, Jews had lived in Germany for sixteen hundred years. At various times during that period, Jews had been intimidated, physically assaulted, and driven from their homes and towns. Some had been killed—all for no reason other than that they were Jewish. For centuries the German people, who were nearly all Christians, scorned, shunned, and abused Jews because they saw Judaism as the enemy of Christian faith. Many German Christians even called Jews "Christ killers."

Anti-Semitism

In the 1800s, a popular notion was that Jews belonged to a distinct ethnic group or race. The journalist Wilhelm Marr coined the term *Semite* to distinguish Jews from other Germans, whom he called Aryans. A

Der Giftpilz

Erzählungen von Ernst Hiemer

Bilder von Fips

number of essays, books, and articles described the different races and claimed to show "scientifically" that the blond Aryan was far superior to the darker Semite. According to the popular literature, the Aryan was noble and good, intellectually gifted, and the bearer of culture. Semites were base and evil, intellectually and morally corrupt, without any culture of their own. They were an inferior race. As the twentieth century approached, racial persecution replaced religious intolerance and acquired a new name: anti-Semitism.

Anti-Semitism was a much more dangerous form of persecution than what had existed prior to the beginning of the twentieth century. If Jews were classified as members of a barely human race, their lives were hardly worthy of existence. Even worse, Jews would poison German culture, pollute the German character, and ultimately destroy Germany itself. There was no hope for Jews. Even if they gave up their religious heritage and traditions, they could not change what they were by birth. They could no longer be ignored as a religious minority, but must be eliminated as a threat to the purity of the Aryan race. The outcome of such thinking was genocide—the systematic murder of a race or people. Eugen Karl Dühring, a University of Berlin professor, philosopher, and economist, wrote that "the duty of the Nordic [Aryan] peoples is to exterminate such parasitic races [Jews] as we exterminate snakes and beasts of prey."[1]

Anti-Semitism or prejudice against Jews even took the form of propaganda, as in this children's book, Der Giftpilz *(The Poisonous Mushroom). This book was published in Germany in the mid-1930s.*

German Nationalism

At the same time as racial anti-Semitism was erupting with hateful pamphlets, posters, and newspapers, a powerful political movement was forming that would fuel the fire of anti-Jewish feelings. German-speaking people, who were scattered among dozens of small European states, began to draw together to form a single, unified nation. The country blazed with a fierce nationalism, an intense passion for all that was German—a passion so extreme that anything even remotely non-German was despised. Jews were now labeled *non-German*. Because they had been "proven" to be ethnically different from "true" Germans, they were considered outsiders, aliens, foreigners. The religious and racial persecution of Jews was infused with a new zeal: political anti-Semitism.

Despite all this, Germany continued to be a more comfortable and safer haven for Jews than many other areas of Europe. Jews had not been expelled from Germany, as they had from other European countries. The persecution that Jews faced in Germany did not compare with the violence that took place in parts of Eastern Europe. Because of this, many Jews throughout Europe had converged on Germany, and the Jewish population in this country rose significantly. This helped fuel the fire that would become anti-Semitism.

Hatred of Jews was everywhere, a part of the social fabric of nineteenth-century Germany. Shelves of newsstands and libraries were lined with titles such as *The Jewish Question, Essay on the Inequality of the Human Races*, and *The Despairing Struggle of the Aryan People with Jewry*. Desks of government officials were cluttered with thousands upon thousands of pamphlets sent to them without charge each year by anti-Semitic groups.[2] The streets of many cities were littered with leaflets, handbills, and posters warning of the Jewish danger. Meeting halls and beer parlors were packed with citizens who belonged to the many organizations and political parties that had formed for the sole purpose of combating anything Jewish—136 of them in 1890.[3] What made this influx of anti-Semitic literature and political organization so surprising is that few Germans supported the radical anti-Semitic parties in the late nineteenth century. Anti-Semitism was supported by a minority of the German people, but it was a growing, and vocal, one. Even with the large volume of anti-Semitic literature and the increasing membership in political organizations, however, few Germans voted for the radical anti-Semitic parties in the late nineteenth century.

Effects of World War I

Germany's defeat in World War I (1914–1918) whipped the white-hot coals of anti-Semitism into flames. The conflict had been a disaster: Two million German soldiers, whose ranks included Jews, had lost their lives. For four years the financial resources and the manpower of the country had been poured into weapons of destruction. The war had cost 164 billion marks.[4] The German mark is a unit of currency worth about twenty-five cents in 1918. And all of it was gone—lost along with the war, the army, and the pride and honor of a nation.

The Treaty of Versailles that officially ended the war was dictated by the victors; Germany had no voice in any of its provisions. The treaty slashed the size of the German military: Only a volunteer army was allowed, and it could never number more than one hundred thousand. No planes, tanks, submarines, or large ships were permitted, so the country was left with no air force and virtually no navy. Germany had to admit total responsibility for causing the war and

A young Adolf Hitler joined thousands of Germans in celebration in Munich at the beginning of World War I. Although Hitler was Austrian, he joined the German Army and achieved the rank of corporal.

pay all the costs the victorious countries had incurred, a figure set at 132 billion marks—in gold, not paper—about $33 billion.[5]

A proud and hurting people who had been humiliated into an unconditional surrender looked for a scapegoat—for someone to blame. Despite the fact that more than one hundred thousand Jews had fought proudly in the German Army, the Jews—already branded as foreigners—were the logical enemy.[6] And at just the moment when the anger, frustration, and hunger of the devastated masses began to demand a target, a little book surfaced that pointed squarely to the hated Jew.

Conspiracy Accusations

The Protocols of the Elders of Zion had been written around 1895 for the Russian czar (emperor) to use to justify punishing revolutionaries in his country. Devised by agents of the Russian secret police, *The Protocols* created a fictional Jewish organization—a secret society that was plotting to take over the world. *The Protocols* were supposedly the actual records of meetings of this secret group. The document claimed to expose a conspiracy of Jews along with bankers, liberals, and others for world domination.

In 1917, during the Bolshevik revolution in Russia, copies of *The Protocols* were used by the government in an attempt to convince people that the revolution was part of a Jewish scheme. Russians escaping the revolution in their country carried *The Protocols* all over the world. Even though the book had been proven undeniably to be a fabrication, it was translated into dozens of languages and sold in every European country, in the United States, and in many Arab-speaking cities. In the early 1900s, only the Bible sold more copies.[7]

The Protocols came to Germany in 1918. Just as the Germans were looking for a way to explain the tragedy of World War I, *The Protocols* gave them the answer: Jews around the world had conspired to destroy Germany so they could rule. *The Protocols* provided an explanation for Germany's defeat: The Jews had stabbed Germany in the back. The Jews were responsible for the forced surrender, the degrading treaty, and the economic chaos that followed the war.

Now Germans had many false reasons to hate Jews. Their religion was opposed to the Christian tradition of the country. They were of an inferior race. They were aliens and therefore threatened the unity of the nation. Finally, they were part of an international conspiracy that was bent on Germany's demise.

By the 1920s and 1930s, the "Jewish Problem" had come to be viewed as a national cancer. The typical German citizen had long been conditioned to accept as fact the motto brandished on the front page of every issue of the newspaper *Der Stürmer*: "The Jews are our misfortune."[8] The 430 anti-Jewish societies[9] and the political candidates who railed against Jews did not create the climate of hatred; they merely reflected the mood of the country.

Violence

The mood of the country darkened even more as economic and social conditions worsened. Expressions of anti-Semitism moved from the social halls and beer parlors to the streets in Germany. Anti-Semitism had become more publicly accepted and more widely practiced. For example, Walter Rathenau was an industrialist who had supplied materials for the German Army in World War I. Appointed minister of reconstruction after the war, he had helped put the broken pieces of the country back together. Then, as foreign minister, he had represented German interests in the international arena. But he was a Jew. Demonstrators marched in the streets, brazenly chanting, "Mow down Walter Rathenau." On June 24, 1922, Rathenau was assassinated.

In 1923, 350 Jews were forcibly driven from the German province of Bavaria. By 1930, random harassment had turned to murder as eight Jews were slain on New Year's Day. During an election campaign later that year, seventy-eight Jews were injured by mob violence. In 1931 alone, at least fifty synagogues and more than one hundred Jewish cemeteries were vandalized and desecrated.[10]

Anti-Semitism Everywhere

Although violence-prone fanatics were in the forefront of the physical attacks, every institution of German life fed the anti-Semitic frenzy. Student organizations in the universities kept Jewish youths from their classrooms by either policy or intimidation. Certain businesses and entire professions closed their doors to Jews. Jews constantly faced persecutions at home, on every level of society.

The centuries of anti-Semitic slander and the decades of racial propaganda had created in the German

After defeat in World War I, more and more Germans turned toward the nationalist parties that claimed to look after the German people first. It was from this atmosphere that the Nazi party rose to power.

mind a picture of the Jew—whether man, woman, or child; skilled physician or common laborer; traditionally devout or Christian convert—as a hideous monster sucking the life blood of the nation. Hatred of Jews had become equated with love for the Fatherland. If any people felt differently, few were courageous enough to speak out against the overwhelming tide of public sentiment. By 1933, anti-Semitism was more than a way of life; it was an economic force, a political cause, and a religious conviction. Jews had become the most hated people in Germany.

No single person created the climate of hate. No single person twisted the truth until an entire nation believed a lie. But one person did make it his personal mission to "whip up and inflame" the anti-Semitism of his countrymen until genocide was the natural, logical, and only possible conclusion.[11] One person had the will and acquired the power to translate warped thoughts and hateful feelings into national policy. One person was able to make the human sacrifice to the God of Race deliberate and massive. That person was Adolf Hitler.

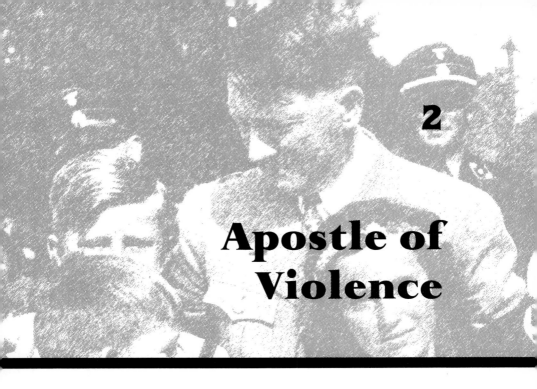

2

Apostle of Violence

Adolf Hitler was a most unlikely leader. The head of the German cause was not German, but Austrian. The champion of German music, art, and literature as the only real culture was a high school dropout. The promoter of the tall, blond, blue-eyed Aryan as the Master Race was of medium height with small eyes and dark hair.

Hitler did not look like a leader. His small frame, quick movements, and tiny mustache reminded people of the well-known clown of silent films, Charlie Chaplin. His physical appearance, according to one expert in the "science" of racial biology, indicated that he was from a "bad race, mongrel." Movements of his eyes and mouth, the expert noted, were "not of a man commanding with full self-control, but betraying insane excitement." The impression he gave was one of "blissful egotism."[1]

Yet huge crowds thronged to Hitler's rallies. Thousands cheered him and millions voted for him. In

1920, one newspaper called him "the most cunning rabble rouser in Munich."[2] Hitler was a powerful and persuasive speaker. He knew what the demoralized, discontented masses of Germany wanted to hear. He told them that their country could be strong again, that "on the ruins of the wretched Germany of today" there could arise "once more a Germany of power and greatness, of freedom and splendor."[3] And they lined up by the hundreds to join the Storm Troops, his private army. He told the crowd they were the jewels of Europe, with "the right to a greater living space than other peoples."[4] And they marched in the streets under his banner. He told them that what prevented them from attaining the lofty dreams to which he said they were entitled, what had created all their misery, was their enemy: the Jewish people. And they attacked their Jewish neighbors with fists, clubs, and knives.

Hitler promised the Germans glory, honor, and jobs. He gave stirring voice to their deepest desire: Germany would be great again once the parasitic Jews were removed from its midst. He knew what the Germans thought and what they felt, and he played to their emotions. Thus he became their leader—their Führer.

Hitler's Youth

Hitler's early years were not exceptional in any way. He was born on April 20, 1889, in Braunau, Austria—a tiny town on the Inn River that formed part of the border with Germany. His mother was a peasant who worked as a housekeeper, and his father, twenty-three years older than his mother, was employed by the Austrian government as a customs official. The couple had to obtain special permission to marry because they were second cousins. Adolf's ancestry is checkered with illegitimacy, abandonment, and at least one other marriage between close relatives.

22

Although Adolf Hitler did not match the image of the tall, blue-eyed Aryan, he was a powerful speaker who promised Germans glory, honor, and jobs. Hitler's fanatical anti-Semitism led the German people to carry out the worst horrors in history.

Hitler's father wanted Adolf to follow in his footsteps, with a career in government service. But as early as age eleven, Adolf had decided to become an artist. Drawing was one of only two subjects in which he scored high grades in secondary school; the other was gymnastics. His secondary school record was so poor his parents had to transfer him to a different school, but after a short time he dropped out of school altogether without graduating. A teacher later described him as "gifted" but said "he lacked self-control and . . . was argumentative, autocratic, self-opinionated and bad-tempered, and unable to submit to school discipline."[5]

Hitler's father died when Adolf was thirteen, and four years later his mother sent him from their home in Linz to Austria's capital, Vienna, to pursue his dream of becoming a painter. Twice he applied to the Vienna Academy of Fine Arts but was rejected as having insufficient talent. He thought of studying architecture, but he lacked a secondary school diploma. So he returned to Linz and was content to let his mother continue to support him.

Although he had not applied himself in school, young Adolf loved to read. His only known friend, August Kubizek,[6] described him as always surrounded by books—mostly stories of Germany's illustrious past and essays on German history and greatness.[7] He spent his later teen years doing little but reading, daydreaming, and listening to operas by the anti-Semitic composer Richard Wagner. But his mother's death when he was nineteen brought his carefree, "comfortable" life to a close.[8]

With little more than a suitcase and a small inheritance, Hitler moved to Vienna and began what he later called "the saddest period in my life."[9] He had no job, no skills, and no connections. For five years he drifted from one day laborer job to another. He shoveled snow, carried suitcases, and sold a few postcard-like paintings. He was always hungry.

And Hitler read. He devoured books on Teutonic (German) myth and legend, pamphlets on race, and articles on politics. He immersed himself in all of the Jew-hating thought of his day. During this time, he later wrote, he made a conscious decision to become an anti-Semite.[10]

In 1913, Hitler moved from Vienna to Munich, Germany. He saw himself—and most of his former countrymen—as Austrian according to geography but German by ethnicity and heritage. In Munich, the capital of the German province of Bavaria, he continued to live as a penniless, untalented, and completely unmotivated vagabond.

World War I was a turning point for the young drifter. At age twenty-five he obtained permission to fight for Germany. Service in the army gave him focus, discipline, and an Iron Cross for bravery, which he wore for the rest of his life. When the war ended in defeat, shame, and political and social turmoil, Hitler finally knew what he wanted to do with his life. "I decided," he later recalled, "to go into politics."[11]

The Nazi Party

In 1919, at age thirty, Adolf Hitler joined the small band of men who called themselves the German Workers' Party. A year later Hitler changed the group's name to the National Socialist German Workers' Party (NSDAP were the German initials). The party was called "Nazi" after the abbreviated form of the first word in its title, *Nazional*. Hitler's devotion to the party and the phenomenal skill he was developing as a speaker propelled him quickly to the organization's top ranks. In 1921, he was elected Führer (leader) of the party.

From the beginning, Hitler molded the Nazi party around two key principles. The first was anti-Semitism. When he helped draft the party's creed, he listed as fundamental tenets the goals that no Jew should be a citizen of Germany and that all Jews who had come to Germany since 1914—more than eighteen thousand

25

people—should be expelled.[12] He called for a "systematic and legal struggle against, and eradication of, what privileges the Jews enjoy." But he noted that the "final objective . . . must be the total removal of all Jews from our midst."[13]

Exactly how Hitler envisioned the removal of the Jews from Germany was hinted at by the second principle of the Nazi party: violence. He spoke of "brutally and ruthlessly . . . tear[ing] out the weeds" of society.[14] He regarded terror as "the most effective political instrument," necessary for crushing resistance.[15] "Terror," he proclaimed, "will always be successful unless opposed by equal terror."[16]

One of the party's instruments of terror and violence was the group of volunteers known as the *Sturmabteilung* (SA), or Storm Troops. The functions of this body of men included guarding Nazi gatherings, disrupting meetings of competing parties, and harassing anyone who opposed Hitler. The Storm Troops were also called Brownshirts because of the color of their uniforms. Many were soldiers who had been unable to find jobs in postwar Germany. Membership in the SA gave them a new fighting cause. And Hitler's speeches blaming all the country's ills on the Jews gave them a new enemy. The Brownshirts flexed their muscle with unprovoked attacks on Jewish citizens and businesses. Aryan Germans, having convinced themselves that Jews were subhuman, looked the other way.

On their arms the Brownshirts wore a symbol of both anti-Semitism and violence. Hitler had selected

Adolf Hitler rose to power and united the German people by making anti-Semitism a national policy. Many Nazi propaganda photos have Hitler posing with young people.

the swastika, a twisted cross, as the emblem of the Nazi party because it suggested to him "the mission of the struggle for the victory of the Aryan man."[17] Although it was centuries old, Hitler had undoubtedly seen the crooked cross on the flags of some Austrian anti-Semitic parties and the helmets of at least one German revolutionary military group. The choice of this ancient pagan symbol mocked both Jews and Christians.

The Nazis did not attempt to hide or disguise their violent anti-Semitism. They shouted it in the streets: "Germany awake! Death to the Jew!" They tacked it on poles and scrawled it across walls: "Jews, perish!"[18] They demonstrated it with random beatings of innocent Jewish citizens. And the people cheered them on.

Beer Hall Putsch

Buoyed by his growing popularity and emboldened by the number of armed men at his command, Hitler attempted to take over Germany in a November 1923 *putsch* (overthrow plot). Hitler's plan was to gain control of the government, the army and police, and the communications and other strategic centers in Munich and then to march to Berlin, the capital, and proclaim a revolution. The attempted coup began in a beer hall when Hitler interrupted a speech by Bavarian State Commissioner Gustav von Kahr to the political and social elite of the state. It gathered momentum when Hitler and several supporters led three thousand Storm Troops to the city center under the banner of the swastika. It ended when one hundred policemen

Hitler was a very popular leader with the young people of Germany. Here young women (top) wave Nazi flags and cheer German troops. Hitler reviews a group of Hitler Youth (below) from a Vienna balcony in 1938.

blocked the marchers' path. In a flurry of bullets, sixteen Nazis and three police officers died, several others were wounded, and Hitler ran away.

Within a few days, all but two of the leaders of the Beer Hall Putsch had been arrested. Before being found guilty of treason and sentenced to five years in prison, Hitler used the trial to place himself in the national spotlight. His eloquent criticism of an unpopular regime, the government installed after World War I, and his defense of his "patriotic" rebellion won him the admiration of many. He spent less than nine months in the Landsberg prison, in a private room with comfortable furnishings, good food, and a continual flow of visitors. He used the time to dictate *Mein Kampf* to Rudolf Hess, one of the two putsch conspirators who had escaped. The book, whose title means "my struggle," presented Hitler's distorted version of his own life, his hate-filled ravings against Jews, and his blueprint for a Nazi Germany.

Hitler emerged from prison with a new strategy. Instead of winning control of the country through armed revolution, he would seize power without breaking any law. It would take longer, he knew, but it would be surer and safer.[19]

Rebuilding the Party

First, he set about rebuilding his political party. When he introduced the Nazi program on February 25, 1920, the party had only sixty members, a figure that would climb to three thousand by the next year. By 1925, the Nazis registered 27,000 people and party membership grew steadily: 49,000 in 1926; 72,000 in 1927; 108,000 in 1928; and 178,000 in 1929.[20]

Then, he shaped the party into one of the dominant features of German life. It had a place for everyone. Men marched as Storm Troops, and women belonged

Adolf Hitler (sixth from left) and his collaborators stand trial for the Beer Hall Putsch, the attempted overthrow of the Weimar government in 1923. Hitler was imprisoned but released shortly thereafter. The Nazi party gained publicity and popularity from this failed overthrow of the government.

to the *N.S. Frauenschaften* (National Socialist Women's League). Fifteen- to eighteen-year-olds joined the Hitler Youth, and younger children were in the *Deutsches Jungvolk* (German youngsters). There were different party organizations for students, teachers, government employees, doctors, lawyers, and artists.

Once Hitler took power, the Nazi party rivaled the national government in size and scope. It was organized into departments that paralleled the bureaus of state—departments of agriculture, justice, labor, economy, and race and culture. There were divisions of foreign affairs and of propaganda. The Nazi machine was much more than a political party and more than a social and cultural club. It was a "state within a state."

In one area the Nazi "state" was actually more powerful than the German nation. The entire country of Germany, under the terms of the Treaty of Versailles, was permitted an army of only one hundred thousand; Hitler's private force was four times that size. The Storm Troops, the military arm of the party, numbered more than four hundred thousand.

From these soldiers, Hitler selected the most fanatical for his personal bodyguard. Called the *Schutzstaffel* (SS), they wore black uniforms and swore an oath of loyalty not to the country or to the party, but to Hitler himself. In 1925, the SS or Black Guard was a small band of loyalists, but it grew until it replaced the brown-shirted SA, both in anti-Semitic fury and in violent brutality.

Gaining Power

Once Hitler had built his party, his next step was to have its members fill every possible seat in the Reichstag, the lawmaking body of the German nation. Before the election of 1928, he saw to it that posters, pamphlets, and newspapers blanketed the country with the Nazi promise of a glorious Germany. He raced feverishly from city to city, personally igniting the masses with his vision of national greatness and his condemnation of Jews. He succeeded in helping his party win 810,000 votes and twelve seats in the

Hitler walks to his car after addressing a rally in Berlin in 1936. As leader of the Nazi Party, Hitler was able to create an army—the Storm Troops (SA)—several times the size of Germany's armed forces.

When the Nazis took over the government, they cracked down on any literature that spoke out against their beliefs. Here a member of the SA burns "un-German" books in Berlin.

legislature. But Hitler hoped for even more. His goals for the next election, two years later, were 3 million votes and fifty seats.[21]

But in October 1929, before that election could take place, the American stock market collapsed and economies all over the world sank into a great depression. German businesses could no longer borrow money from the United States or other countries, and no nation had enough money to buy German products. Banks failed. Factories closed their operations, and small businesses shut down. Six million Germans found themselves unemployed. It was a time of deep misery and dark despair for the German people, but a tremendous opportunity for Hitler. He convinced many of the starving, desperate electorate that his was the party of hope. In 1930 the Nazis received 6.4 million votes and 107 seats in the Reichstag. In 1932 they won 13.7 million votes and 230 seats.

Hitler had acquired so much power, legally, that the eighty-six-year-old president, Paul von Hindenburg, appointed him the nation's chancellor on January 30, 1933. It was not a position of absolute authority: He shared the reins of the country with others in the cabinet and, technically, he served at the aging president's will. But for all practical purposes, Hitler was now in charge of Germany.

Hitler pompously proclaimed that his accession to the chancellory marked the dawn of a new and glorious period in Germany's history: the Third Reich. The first Reich (government or dynasty) was the Holy Roman Empire, from 800 to 1806 A.D. The second was a new empire created by Chancellor Otto von Bismark, which lasted from 1871 until defeat in World War I in 1918. The Third Reich, Hitler promised, would be like the first: It would last a thousand years.[22]

On the night of Hitler's appointment, thousands of Storm Troops celebrated their Führer's victory with a boisterous torchlight parade through the streets of Berlin that lasted for hours. But in Jewish homes the mood was dark. A boy who was ten years old at the time recalled coming home from a day of innocent play to learn the news. The man who had proclaimed that war against the Jews was "the work of the Lord" was now the most powerful man in the country. "When . . . we heard that Hitler had become Chancellor," he remembered, "everybody shook. As kids of ten we shook."[23]

The trembling that began that day in 1933 grew in intensity until it became a violent convulsion that shook the nation to its very core and reverberated throughout the entire world.

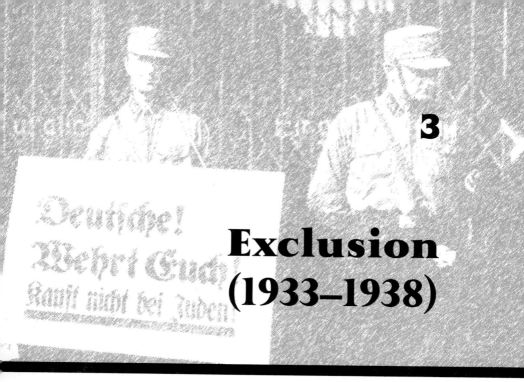

Exclusion (1933–1938)

3

Once the torches of the victory parade were extinguished, Chancellor Hitler began the task of expanding his power. Although he was committed to the appearance of gaining control through legal means, he had no qualms about bending the rules to obtain greater power. The instruments he used for manipulating the law were the same ones he had used before: violence and deception.

On the night of February 27, 1933, less than two months after Hitler took a solemn oath to defend his country, the Reichstag building was set on fire. A man the Nazis labeled as a Communist, who was known to be a pyromaniac, was found with matches and gasoline, but evidence is strong that Nazi Storm Troops actually engineered the blaze. Hitler convinced many, including the ailing President Hindenburg, that the Reichstag fire was the beginning of a Communist attempt to topple his government. The day after the fire, Hindenburg signed an emergency decree "For the Protection of

People and State" that did away with most of the freedoms guaranteed by the constitution. Citizens no longer had the right to freedom of speech, freedom of assembly, or freedom of the press. They could be searched at any time, have their mail opened, or have their telephone conversations monitored. Those accused of crimes that the Nazis considered threatening to the security of the state—crimes as simple as disturbing the peace—could be punished by death.

Under the emergency decree, Hitler could brand almost anyone as a Communist or other such danger and have that person arrested. Indeed, in the first few weeks following the Reichstag fire, four thousand Communists and a host of other enemies of Nazism were taken into custody.[1] Thus Hitler could, perfectly legally, remove from positions of influence those who opposed him.

The Enabling Act

Just weeks after Nazi vandalism and lies convinced the president to issue the emergency decree of February 28, Hitler asked the Reichstag to pass the Enabling Act. Officially called the "Law for Removing the Distress of People and Reich," it gave the cabinet—which Hitler headed—complete legislative authority for four years. Hitler knew he did not have the two-thirds majority needed to pass the measure. So he exercised the executive powers of the emergency decree and his personal authority as leader of the Storm Troops to scare away or imprison people who would vote against the legislation. He built the first of what would be hundreds of concentration camps at Dachau, just outside Munich, to house and intimidate the political enemies of the Nazis. Dachau was ready to receive prisoners the day before the vote on the Enabling Act was to be taken. Members of the Reichstag could not, according to law,

The Reichstag, Germany's main government building, was set on fire the night of February 27, 1933. Hitler used the burning of the Reichstag as an excuse for persecuting political foes and enemies of the state. Today, it is believed that Hitler intentionally ordered the building to be burned.

be arrested, but when the measure came before the legislative body, eighty-one Communist and twenty-six Socialist lawmakers were absent. By a vote of 441 to 94, the Enabling Act was passed on March 23, 1933, giving Hitler absolute control of Germany.

Every legal victory for Hitler had been accompanied by the sadistic cruelty of the Brownshirts, the legally sanctioned harassment and even murder of innocent citizens. In England and the United States, reports of the brutality in Germany prompted a threat of a boycott of German goods—people would refuse to buy products made in Germany. Even though the Western nations did not carry out their threat, Hitler reacted by creating a national enemy upon which to blame the foreign disdain: the Jews.

Boycott

The Nazi newspaper issued a full-page call in its March 29, 1933, edition for a nationwide boycott of "Jewish shops, Jewish goods, Jewish doctors, and Jewish lawyers."[2] Posters went up immediately in cities throughout the country accusing "international Jewry" of fabricating stories of atrocities in order to "increase poverty and unemployment" and "to fight against Germany." Nazi propagandists twisted the facts, appealing to all "German men and women to observe this boycott"[3] as the only way to defend themselves against disaster at the hands of "the world enemy."[4]

On April 1, 1933—a Saturday, the Jewish Sabbath— SA squads stormed through the cities of Germany, painting black swatches with yellow Stars of David across the doors and windows of thousands of factories, stores, and cafes. They drew swastikas and painted messages such as "Jew, die." With an organized precision that was to become characteristic of Nazi terror, at exactly 10 A.M. Brownshirts positioned themselves in front of Jewish establishments with signs advising "Germans" not to enter. The first step in excluding Jews from German life had been taken.

Although surprised and outraged by the growing fervor of Nazi opposition, the majority of Jews thought that Hitler's power or his resolve against them would weaken, and they would return to the status that they had prior to the Versailles Treaty. Even the editor of a German-Jewish newspaper encouraged them to "wear the yellow badge with pride" instead of shrinking from their Jewishness in fear.[5] The prevailing belief was that this period of extreme anti-Semitism would soon pass. Nevertheless, in 1933, Hitler's first year as chancellor, thirty-seven thousand Jews fled Germany.[6]

For the 525,000 who remained, the boycott of Jewish businesses was only the beginning of exclusion from society. Six days later, on April 7, an order was issued demanding the "retirement" of all government workers who were not "of Aryan descent." Within days, other laws were passed that barred non-Aryans from practicing law, serving as judges or jurors, and practicing medicine or dentistry in state facilities. The Law Against the Overcrowding of German Schools set limits on the number of Jews who could be enrolled in educational institutions. New laws forbade universities to employ Jewish professors and kept Jews from performing in live theater or in movies. By the end of 1933, Jews could not work in radio, farming, or

The SA were active in the efforts to boycott Jewish businesses. The signs read, "Germans, defend yourselves against the Jewish atrocity propaganda, buy only at German Shops!" and "Germans, defend yourselves, buy only at German Shops."

teaching. Hitler's legislative dictatorship permitted him to move forward rapidly.

The only restraint slowing Hitler's progress was soon removed. On August 2, 1934, President Hindenburg died. Three hours after his death, the people were told that, on the previous day, the cabinet had enacted a law joining the offices of president and chancellor. Hitler was now not only the nation's chief legislator, but also its chief executive and Commander-in-Chief of its armed forces. He now assumed the title *Führer und Reichskanzler* (leader and reichschancellor) and was the absolute dictator of Germany. Again Jews trembled—and with good reason.

Nuremberg Laws

The Nazi program of excluding Jews from the economic, social, and political life of their country could now proceed unchallenged. The next step in this program was the passage of the Nuremberg Laws, which had been announced at a party rally held in the city of Nuremberg on September 15, 1935.

There were two Nuremberg Laws, reinforced by thirteen supplementary decrees passed over a period of eight years. One of the original two was the Law for the Protection of German Blood and Honor. It forbade marriage and any sexual relations between Jews and Germans. It denied Jews the right to hire German women under the age of forty-five as servants and prohibited Jews from flying the German flag. The Reich Citizenship Law differentiated between citizens and subjects. It declared that only persons of German blood—and Jewish blood was not German—were citizens. Others could be only subjects, which meant they were entitled to the protection of the government but none of its privileges.

Joseph Goebbels played an instrumental role in the rise to power of the Nazis. He served as the minister of propaganda and used his position to influence the German people to embrace the Nazi ideology of anti-Semitism.

The first supplementary decree, published just one month later, removed any question about who was considered a Jew. A Jew was someone with three Jewish grandparents or someone with two Jewish grandparents who belonged to the Jewish religious community or was married to a Jew or was a child of a Jew.

The flood of legislation was the most blatant attempt to exclude Jews, but not the most common or the most effective. Physical violence was still a powerful instrument of Nazi policy. In a bloody purge, Hitler had replaced most of the Storm Troops with the savagely brutal SS and a state secret police force that was not subject to any law or court—the _Geheime Staatspolizei_, or Gestapo for short. These two groups taunted and tormented Jews wherever they encountered them. They used the Laws of Race and Citizenship to accuse Jews of crimes and take their property.

Most German citizens cooperated in the persecution of Jews. Factory owners dismissed Jewish employees. Merchants refused to sell to Jewish customers. Housewives would not buy goods from Jewish stores. Jewish people were forced to "Aryanize" their businesses—sell them to racially pure Germans for a fraction of their value.

Some Jews coped with their exclusion primarily by turning inward, usually to their religious communities, called kehillot. When their youth were expelled from universities and secondary schools and their children ridiculed in elementary schools, the kehillot established their own educational centers. When they were driven from the arts, they created their own Culture Association that performed operas, concerts, and plays and sponsored art exhibits and other activities. When books by Jewish authors were burned in huge public bonfires, they continued at twenty-five publishing houses of their own.[7] When their jobs or businesses were taken from them, the kehillot fed them, loaned them money, and tried to help them find new ways of earning a living. They hoped the storm would pass.

But the storm did not pass; it worsened. More and more repressive measures were imposed against Jews in 1938. They were forced to add distinctively Jewish names to their own names: "Israel" for males and "Sarah" for females—so they could be easily identified for the mass arrests that were secretly planned. They

One way that Nazis persecuted Jews was to publicly embarrass them. For instance, this Nazi is forcing a German Jew to sweep the pavement with a broom.

had to register their property—so it could be confiscated more easily.

The repressive laws were accompanied by acts of terror. In June 1938, the main synagogue in Munich was destroyed—burned to the ground—at Hitler's personal order.[8] Synagogues in at least two other cities were also demolished. A few days later fifteen hundred Jews with police records, many for very minor "crimes" such as traffic violations, were rounded up and taken to concentration camps.

Kristallnacht

As demoralizing as these acts of persecution were, they were small compared with the sadistic terror unleashed against the Jews in November 1938. The pretext was the assassination of Ernst vom Rath, a German official, by Herschel Grynszpan, a young Jew angered over the treatment of his parents. While he was a student in France, Herschel's family was forcibly and harshly deported from Germany to their native Poland. The boy's father, Zindel, described his family's ordeal in a postcard to his son. The angry seventeen-year-old marched to the German embassy in Paris and shot vom Rath, the first German he could find. Finally, Hitler had the excuse he needed to act. The assassination would become the catalyst for massive riots, conducted under the guise of "spontaneous reactions."

On the evening of November 9, men of the SS, Storm Troops, and Gestapo—all dressed in civilian clothes and armed with axes, hammers, crowbars, clubs, and fire bombs—spilled onto streets all over Germany. They smashed windows and splintered the walls of Jewish homes and shops. They hurled the contents of the shattered buildings—furniture, merchandise, and even the people inside—into the roads that were littered with glass, and they took anything that was not broken. They tore into synagogues, defiled the holy books and articles inside, and then set the sacred buildings on fire. They dragged Jewish families from their homes and beat them. When Kristallnacht—the Night of Broken Glass—was over, 1300 synagogues and 171 homes had been burned, 76 synagogues were destroyed, 7,500 shops

---

Kristallnacht, the Night of Broken Glass, left destruction and ruin at Jewish shops, homes, and synagogues throughout Germany. Store windows were broken (top), homes destroyed, and synagogues were burned (bottom).

had been looted,[9] 91 Jews were reported dead[10] and 36 seriously wounded. At least 30,000 Jews had been arrested and taken to concentration camps.

As if the highly organized, barbaric orgy of destruction were not inhumane enough for the Nazi government, the Jews were forced to pay for the damage their persecutors had inflicted. On November 12, 1938, a fine of one billion marks (the equivalent of $400 million) was levied against the Jewish community. Other penalties followed within days. All Jewish children were forbidden to attend public schools. Jews could not be treated in non-Jewish hospitals, could not enter places of recreation, could not drive cars or use public transportation. By the end of 1938, the exclusion of Jews from every facet of German life was complete. Jews had no rights, no property, and no protection. The second stage of the Holocaust had already begun.

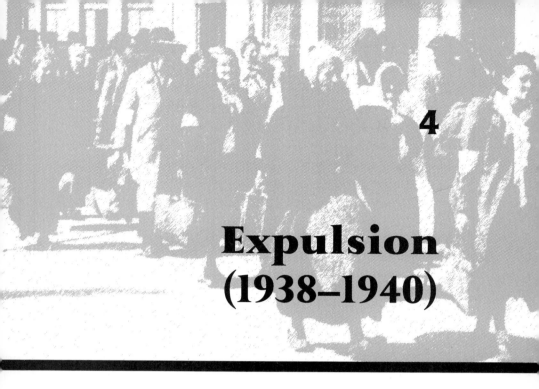

4

Expulsion (1938–1940)

The relentless persecution of the Jews by the Nazi government had one objective: the "total removal of all Jews from our midst."[1] Hitler's aim was for the Reich to be *Judenrein* (cleansed of Jews). The officially instigated acts of terror were intended to frighten Jews into leaving Germany. The confiscation of businesses was meant to make remaining in Germany economically impossible. Even the initial internment in concentration camps was part of the scheme: Prisoners would be released upon their promise to emigrate. The plan was working. By the end of 1938 nearly half the nation's five hundred thousand Jews had found refuge in other countries.

Expulsion From Austria

The success of the expulsion stage was largely due to the work of one man in Austria, Karl Adolf Eichmann. In March 1938, using the threat of force, Hitler succeeded in annexing Austria, making it part of

Germany and adding some two hundred thousand Austrian Jews to his domain. Hitler did not meet with much resistance in annexing Austria, because many Austrians felt they shared a common heritage with Germans and welcomed their inclusion into the larger German state. Eichmann, an SS officer, was given command of the Office for Jewish Emigration in Austria. His task was to get as many Jews to leave Austria as possible, and he tore into his assignment with relish.

First, he simplified the exit process, making it easy for Jews to emigrate. Then, he "encouraged" their departure through physical violence, intimidation, and the threat of imprisonment. He rounded up wealthy Jews, Aryanized all they owned (that is, confiscated their property and their wealth), and used their money to pay for the emigration of poorer Jews. Years later, one Jewish leader described Eichmann's operation as

> a flour mill tied in with a bakery. You put a Jew in at one end . . . [and] he comes out at the other with no money, no rights, only a passport saying: You must leave the country within two weeks; otherwise you will go to a concentration camp.[2]

Eichmann's methods were harsh but efficient. In the eight months from the annexation of Austria in March through the arrests following Kristallnacht in November, Germany expelled nineteen thousand Jews while Austria exiled fifty thousand.

Adolf Eichmann headed the Department for Jewish Affairs in the Gestapo and was responsible for enacting many of the goals of the Final Solution. He was the leading figure in the deportation of 3 million Jews to extermination camps.

But voluntary emigration on such a massive scale carried with it one major problem: Where could so many people go? On July 6, 1938, United States president Franklin D. Roosevelt called together representatives of thirty-two nations in Evian, France, to discuss the question. However, the conference offered no solutions. Most delegates were reluctant to accept Jewish refugees because, although Jews could leave Germany, they were not permitted to take any money with them and would thus be economic burdens. Some countries reduced the number of immigrants they would receive, and others toughened the requirements for entering. Previously, England had allowed Jewish refugees to settle in Palestine, its colony in the Middle East; now England put a tight cap on immigration to Palestine. The representative from Australia closed his nation's doors to Jewish refugees with the terse statement: "As we have no racial problem, we are not desirous of importing one."[3] The Swiss delegate expressed similar feelings, proclaiming that Switzerland "has as little use for these Jews as has Germany."[4]

Thus the Nazi plan to rid Germany of its Jews through voluntary emigration ground to a halt toward the end of 1938. But the refusal of other countries to admit Germany's Jews and the reluctance of the Jews to leave the land that had been their home for generations did not keep Hitler from pushing forward with his objective. If the Jews would not leave on their own, they could be forced to go.

Forced Emigration

The first forced emigration was the expulsion of Polish Jews from Germany in October 1938. The government of Poland, itself anti-Semitic, had failed to renew the passports of Polish Jews living in Germany. The German government schemed to return the unwanted

Polish citizens to their native country before their passports expired. The Gestapo hastily collected about seventeen thousand Jews—men, women, and children—and loaded them onto railroad cars. The trains carried them to the edge of Germany and dumped them at the border. There they were robbed of all but their passports and ten marks each and driven with whips into Poland.

Among those left stranded in Poland's no-man's land was the Grynszpan family, and this deportation was the event that triggered Herschel's assassination of Ernst vom Rath. Hitler turned vom Rath into a martyr and Grynszpan into a villain. This incident was the initial link in the chain of events that led to Kristallnacht.

The expulsion phase of the Holocaust resulted in the removal of the entire Jewish population of cities to the death and concentration camps.

Even with the growing persecution, many Jews were hesitant to leave the only homes they had ever known. The majority of those who emigrated moved to neighboring European countries, clinging to the hope that when the world woke from the "bad dream" of Nazism they could return to the land and the lives they had before Hitler turned everything upside down. But throughout much of Europe, Jews could not escape their tormentors.

Expulsions From Czechoslovakia

After Austria, Hitler turned eastward to Czechoslovakia. He incorporated it into the Reich slowly, piece by piece. He convinced the leaders of other countries that the millions of ethnic Germans living in Czechoslovakia should be and wanted to be part of Germany. At a conference in Munich on September 29, 1938, England, France, and Italy signed an agreement with Hitler: They promised not to object to Germany annexing the Sudetenland—the industrial, mountainous, northwestern area of Czechoslovakia—and Hitler promised to make no further demands. But lies had always been the Führer's method of operation, and at 6:00 A.M. on March 15, 1939, his armies marched without resistance into the Czechoslovakian provinces of Bohemia and Moravia. That evening, Hitler himself rode triumphantly into Prague, the capital, declaring that "Czechoslovakia has ceased to exist."[5] And more than one hundred twenty thousand Jews in Czechoslovakia, including many refugees from Germany and Austria, trembled.

They trembled with good reason. Adolf Eichmann, the SS bureaucrat who had already succeeded in banishing fifty thousand Jews from Austria, was sent to Prague. Eichmann set for himself a goal of expelling seventy thousand Jews a year, making what was once Czechoslovakia *Judenrein* in less than two years.

To achieve this aim, Eichmann used a technique that was to later characterize every strategy of the Holocaust: He forced the leaders of the Jewish people to be instruments of their own demise. He demanded that the local Jewish organization—the Jewish Community Council—deliver to him two hundred Jews each day for deportation. If any could not afford to pay the expenses of their passage out of the Reich, the council was required to come up with the money somehow. When anyone on the council objected, Eichmann's response was cold: "If you do not get these Jews out of the country, I will order the arrest of three hundred men per day and I will send them to [concentration camps] Dachau and Merkelgrün, where I am sure they will become very enthusiastic about emigration."[6]

Living Space

Usually the Jewish Council met its deportation quota. All the Jews throughout the Czech provinces had been ordered to move into the capital, and from there it was a short trip to the railroad cars. But the trains were stalled on the tracks. Nearly every country was closed to Jewish refugees. There was no place to discard these unwanted people except to the east. Some fled to Poland in the north, while others were able to escape southward to Hungary.[7] However, these countries would provide only a temporary refuge for Jews, since Hitler already planned to annex these lands, as well.

Hitler believed that Germany was not big enough to comfortably support its citizens. The Master Race needed greater *lebensraum*—living space. Indeed, Hitler said, their superiority entitled them to move beyond the restrictions of their artificial borders because "only a sufficiently large space on this earth can assure the independent existence of a people."[8] His plan was for all of Europe from Germany eastward—primarily Poland

and the Soviet Union—to be filled with Germans and Germans only. What of the people living in these lands? To Hitler, Poles and Russians were inferior races, little better than Jews. As such, they did not deserve the vast territory that the Germans needed. They would simply have to be removed. Many years earlier, in *Mein Kampf*, the book he wrote in prison, Hitler had clearly announced his intent to stretch the Reich across Poland and into Russia. And he easily justified his aim. "Land awaits the people who have the strength to acquire it and the diligence to cultivate it,"[9] Hitler had proclaimed.

World War II Begins

The German people had the necessary conquering force in 1939. Hitler had completely ignored the Treaty of Versailles, which had kept Germany almost totally disarmed, and had been brazenly rebuilding his country's military might. No European country stopped him because they did not want to risk war again. Some of the European leaders were glad, at first, to have a country opposed to communism between themselves and the Soviet Union. Hitler had added warships and submarines to the tiny navy the treaty permitted. He had built up an air force, which was completely forbidden by the treaty, and had begun to draft young men into the army, creating a force greater than five times the one hundred thousand soldiers the treaty allowed. All this was in addition to the domestic forces he commanded: the SS, the SD, and the Gestapo.

Jews already weak from disease or lack of food were often forced onto death marches by the Germans. Many of these victims, marching from Dachau to Wolfratshausen, would perish during the march. Most of the others would be executed upon arrival at their destination.

The massive rearmament was financed largely with funds confiscated from the Nazi enemies. Accounts of foreigners in German banks and money seized from political prisoners, especially Jews, were used to finance weapons production. The navy was built largely from dues required of the workers who built it. The director of the country's economy, Dr. Hjalmar Schacht, borrowed heavily from other nations and put the money into the arms industry.[10] Thus in 1939 Hitler had the military might to claim the "living space" he wanted across Germany's borders.

But Hitler did not move recklessly into Poland. He realized that England and France felt threatened by his easy takeovers of Austria and Czechoslovakia and were trying to talk Josef Stalin, the leader of the Soviet Union, into forming an alliance with them. Stalin had faced difficulties in forging alliances with France and Britain, both of whom feared communism more than fascism. Therefore, Stalin was the only remaining leader with whom Hitler could reach an agreement. But if Stalin did reach an agreement with these western nations, Germany would have enemies on two fronts: England and France in the west and the Soviet Union in the east. Hitler's plan was to conquer Poland without interference, then defeat both England and France, then turn on the Soviet Union and destroy it, too. On August 23, 1939, before any other country could act, Hitler and Stalin surprised the world with an announcement of a nonaggression pact between Germany and the Soviet Union: The two countries agreed not to fight each other. Now Hitler's troops could march into Poland without fear of attack from the Soviet Union to the east.

Nine days later, at the first light of day on Friday morning, September 1, 1939, German tanks swept across the Polish border with guns blazing. German warplanes bombed bridges, military targets, and cities and shot at fleeing men, women, and children. The railroad cars carrying troops to the front bore demeaning caricatures of Jews and the words: "We're off to Poland—to trash the Jews."[11]

Behind the army came the *Einsatzgruppen*, the SD "action groups" or strike forces of the security police. The task of these twenty-five hundred political soldiers was to seek out the enemies of Germany, which included political refugees, Communists, religious leaders, and Jews. Following the German Army as it advanced, the *Einsatzgruppen* at first arrested enemies of the state, but soon began to systematically murder thousands of Jews and others. In the first two months of the occupation, six thousand Polish Jewish soldiers were killed and five thousand Jewish civilians were murdered.[12] Those who survived were cruelly mocked and tortured. Beards were shaved off or plucked out. Old men were made to clean latrines with their bare hands, their prayer shawls, and other sacred items. Photographs were taken of Jewish men being forced to pull cartloads of German soldiers and of Jewish women dodging bullets as they ran from burning synagogues.

By the time Warsaw, the last holdout, finally surrendered on September 27, 1939, the swastika waved over the western half of Poland and the Russian flag flew over the eastern half. In accordance with secret terms of the agreement signed a month earlier by Hitler and Stalin, Germany took much of Poland and the Soviet Union claimed the rest, together with the Baltic states of Estonia, Latvia, and Lithuania. Hitler would later turn on his Soviet ally, but for now Germany's takeover of Poland gave the Aryan people both "living space" and a place to deport their unwanted Jews.

The Jews of Poland

Hitler divided the newly acquired territory into two sections. The portion immediately adjacent to Germany was annexed, or incorporated, into the Reich. Called the Warthegau, this land was to be "cleansed" of its Jews and its Poles and resettled by Germans. The unincorporated eastern portion, known as the General Government, was to serve as the dumping ground for the expelled people.

The task of "Germanizing" the Warthegau and two other annexed areas belonged to Heinrich Himmler, the head of all the police forces of the Reich: the State Gestapo and the many divisions of the Nazi SS. To his other titles was added "Reich Commissar for the Strengthening of German Folkdom." Himmler entrusted the details of the operation to Reinhard Heydrich, leader of the Reich Security Main Office, the Criminal Police, and the SD. The murderous *Einsatzgruppen* was Heydrich's brainchild. So the expulsion of 650,000 Jews of western Poland, now part of Germany, and of all the Jews remaining in Germany became the responsibility of the most brutal arm of Hitler's government.

Immediately upon receiving his orders, on September 21, 1939, Heydrich issued a directive to his *Einsatzgruppen* officers entitled "The Jewish Question in the Occupied Territory." The written order alluded to a secret "final aim" without saying exactly what that aim was. Heydrich commanded his men to remove all Jews

Mobile groups of SS or police called Einsatzgruppen *followed invading German armies, capturing or killing Jews in the conquered territories. Here a soldier prepares to shoot a Ukraninan Jew kneeling on the edge of a mass grave.*

Reinhard Heydrich was the head of the Nazi Security Police and controlled the fate of the enemies of the Third Reich. He was responsible for the elimination of those deemed undesirable to Germany.

as quickly as possible, on freight cars, to the General Government. Once in the General Government, the Jews were to be herded into a few large cities on or near railroad lines "so as to facilitate subsequent measures." Heydrich did not specify what the "subsequent measures" were, but he made it clear that the deportation and concentration were not the final aim, but "the stages leading to the fulfillment of this final aim."[13]

Between October and December 1939, the official policy and primary action of the Nazi government regarding the Jews was expulsion into eastern Poland. Like every other Nazi policy toward Jews, this "resettlement" was carried out with savage brutality. By the thousands, Jews were herded into trains without food or water. When the sealed railroad cars were opened, children were found frozen to death. Others died of starvation soon after arrival. Many were left in areas so desolate there were no buildings, food, or water. Some were forced to cross rivers where there were no boats, using only flimsy boards, and under the watch of the Gestapo.[14]

One by one, the cities and provinces of Germany and the annexed territories began to be declared *Judenfrei*—Jew free. An official document compiled in 1941 reported that 1.2 million Poles and 300,000 Jews had been removed from the incorporated area of Poland and 497,000 Germans had taken their place.[15] The expulsion stage had been largely successful. The problem now was what to do with the 2.5 million Jews in the General Government. There was no place left to put them.

Hans Frank, the Nazi governor of the unincorporated eastern region of Poland, asked himself the same question in his diary: "We cannot shoot 2,500,000 Jews, neither can we poison them. We shall have to take steps, however, designed to extirpate [completely destroy] them in some way—and this will be done."[16]

Little did he dream that Hitler *could* try to shoot or poison 2,500,000 Jews. Hitler and his followers could devise savage ways to rid themselves and the Reich of more than twice that number. Hitler's plan—what Heydrich called the "final aim"—would follow in two more stages.

5

Enclosure (1940–1942)

The third stage of the Holocaust was enclosure: the walling off of Jews away from their non-Jewish neighbors in labor camps and ghettos. Reinhard Heydrich's September 21, 1939, decree made it clear that enclosure was a temporary policy, a short-term measure necessary for eventual implementation of the yet to be revealed "final aim."

The groundwork for the segregation of Jews was laid in late 1939. In accordance with Heydrich's directive, the Jews who were expelled to the General Government were concentrated in specified locations. Any Jews living in rural areas were required to move to designated cities. Even before these crowded streets were closed off and policed, they were already ghettos—inhabited by Jews alone.

From the very beginning of the German occupation of Poland, the Jews in Poland were allowed to live only to serve their conquerors. Their only value to Germany lay in their material possessions and their ability to work. The Nazis took both for themselves. Any Jewish property that any German wanted was his for the taking. No one stopped the daily raids of soldiers and SS on Jewish shops and homes. Furniture, clothing, artwork, jewelry—anything and everything of value was carted away. When one mother pleaded that a small bed be left for her child, she was told that "a Jewish child does not need a bed."[1]

The heartless, officially sanctioned plunder of Jewish goods was soon given the legitimacy of law. A series of decrees stripped Jews in occupied Poland of nearly everything but the clothes they were wearing. A Defense Tax was levied on all Poles to cover the army's costs in "saving" Poland from the Soviet Union. Access to any bank account listed under a Jewish name was blocked. One order demanded that all Jewish property, from land and businesses to personal belongings, had to be registered. On its heels came another edict: that the property of the Jews be transferred to the Reich government. Hermann Göring, second in power to Hitler and the official in charge of economic matters for the entire Nazi empire, justified these actions: "There must be removed from the territory of the Government General all raw materials, scrap, machines, etc., which are of any use for the German war economy. Enterprises which are not absolutely necessary for the meagre maintenance of the bare existence of the population must be transferred to Germany."[2] Thus Jewish factories, shops, and land enriched Nazi leaders, and Jewish household and personal belongings filled the houses of German citizens being resettled in the annexed provinces.

Forced Labor

Once the Jews were deprived of their material possessions, all they had left of value to the Nazis was their physical strength. This, too, was exploited from

the outset. Jews were snatched on the streets or dragged from their homes and forced to perform all sorts of mindless tasks. They were made to clear streets of the debris that remained from the German invasion, clean the apartments of German officials, scrub the floors of offices that had once belonged to Jews. They were seldom given adequate materials with which to work. Often Jewish women were ordered to use their underclothes or their blouses as cleaning rags.

The kidnapping of Polish Jews for work assignments had been spontaneous and indiscriminate at first, but it was made mandatory by the Forced Labor Decree of October 26, 1939. This law stated that all Jews between the ages of fourteen and sixty living in the General Government were obliged to spend two years working for the officers of the Reich—a term that could be extended if necessary.

To add to their humiliation and to make it easier to work them and harass them, the Jews in several communities were required to wear yellow Stars of David on their coats. On November 23, 1939, Governor Hans Frank issued a decree that all Jews in the General Government over the age of ten must display blue, six-pointed stars on white, four-inch armbands on their right arms. It was not until two years later that the remaining Jews in Germany were made to wear the distinctive emblem. All those wearing the badge on their arms or their coats could expect to be beaten at random, robbed of all they owned, and worked to the brink of death or beyond.

This Jewish girl is in hiding in the Netherlands. She is standing under a sign that warns, in Dutch, "Jews not allowed."

The *Judenrat*

In addition to the concentration of Jews in specific localities, the plunder of all Jewish wealth, and the assignment of Jews to forced labor, only one other measure was necessary before the policy of enclosure could be fully implemented: the establishment of a Jewish government to enforce the Nazi decrees. The German authorities were masters of indirect control. In every measure of cruelty against their enemies, they used the very people they were exploiting to carry out their plans. Just as the Jewish Councils in Germany, Austria, and Czechoslovakia administered the expulsions of Jews from those countries, so in Poland councils were formed that would execute German orders in the forced labor camps and the ghettos. This form of self-government was known as the *Judenrat*. It was responsible for the "dirty work" that was ordered by the Germans. Its purpose was to divert the people's anger and hate from their Nazi oppressors to the Jewish instruments of those oppressors.

Each *Judenrat* in towns of less than ten thousand people consisted of twelve men; those in larger cities had twenty-four. Although members were supposed to be elected, they were actually appointed by local German authorities. The *Judenrat* was charged with registering all Jewish residents, collecting taxes and fees, and delivering daily quotas of workers. The position of the *Judenrat* was an impossible one. On the one hand, the Jews expected the council to stand up for their welfare. On the other hand, the Germans used the council to abuse and enslave the Jews.

With a *Judenrat* in place in every Jewish community, the enclosure of 2 million Polish Jews could begin. The isolation of Jews from their countrymen took two forms: forced labor camps and ghettos.

Jews in the Warsaw ghetto of Poland were forced to build the walls that would confine them. In some cases, gravestones from Jewish cemeteries were used to build these walls, adding further humiliation to Jews.

Labor Camps

The forced work camps served two purposes. First, they eased the labor shortage a widening war brought to Germany. Second, they hastened the unspoken "final aim"—the extermination of the Jewish people—through the "natural deaths" of tens of thousands.

Several of the first work camps were attached to concentration camps, which were originally built not for Jews, but for political prisoners. Some were placed near the cities with the largest concentrations of Jews. Others were located where specific jobs needed to be done. For example, thirty thousand Jews were isolated in camps along the new border with the Soviet Union, where they dug miles of trenches to guard against some future Soviet attack. Three camps built in Poland were later transformed into annihilation centers: Treblinka, fifty miles from Warsaw; Majdanek, on the edge of Lublin; and Auschwitz, not far from Krakow.

Inmates of the forced labor camps performed a variety of backbreaking jobs. They cleared forests of trees and drained marshes to prepare land for buildings. They built roads, fortifications, and new camps. They dug rocks from the sides of mountains, plowed abandoned farmland, and harvested crops. Many were hired out to civilian companies and the profit from their labor lined the pockets of their SS overseers. By the end of 1940, 125 labor camps were in operation throughout the General Government and the Warthegau.[3]

Ghettos

The fate of those Polish Jews not in labor camps was no better. A deliberate attempt to enclose all the Jews in tiny, crowded, guarded sections of a few major cities was begun in earnest in 1940. Although two ghettos had been established earlier—Piotrkow on October 28, 1939, and Radomsko on December 20, 1939—they were "open" ghettos, from which some movement was permitted. The ghettos built in 1940 were closed ghettos; they were surrounded by walls that made

Nazi leaders decided to concentrate all the Jews into confined areas of cities called ghettos. Eventually, Jews were literally walled into the ghettos, as shown here in Krakow, Poland. Tens of thousands of Jews died in ghettos due to disease, malnutrition, and freezing temperatures.

entry and exit nearly impossible. The first closed ghetto was in the large, industrial city of Lodz.

Plans for completely enclosing the one hundred sixty thousand Jews of Lodz had been in place for months. On February 8, 1940, in a "single stroke," all Jews in the city were forcibly and hurriedly moved to a small, dilapidated area of less that two square miles. A barbed-wire fence circled the teeming enclave and the *Judenrat* was commanded to form a police force to guard entry and exit. By April 30, no one was permitted to leave without the permission of German authorities.

More than twenty other ghettos were formed that same year. The largest, in Warsaw, took more than eight months to complete. It began in March, when an outbreak of typhus struck the northern part of the city. The Germans quickly quarantined that section and commanded the *Judenrat* to build eight-foot-high concrete walls to contain the epidemic. The Jews not only had to build the walls, but also had to pay for them. In September all non-Jewish Poles living in the "infected" area were moved out. On October 3, the Jewish feast of Rosh Hashanah, the order was issued that every Jew in Warsaw had to move into the ghetto area. With only the items they could carry in their arms or pull in a wagon or cart, nearly half a million Jews crowded into the buildings in the hundred-block section, six to nine people to a room. In a final blow, on November 15, the twenty-two gates to the ghetto were closed, covered with barbed wire, and guarded by Germans with guns. The top of the eleven-mile length of the wall was studded with broken glass. One resident described the shock of the closure:

> There was no way out any more. . . . Suddenly, the realization struck us. What had been, up till now, seemingly unrelated parts—a piece of wall here, a

blocked-up house there, another piece of wall somewhere else—had overnight been joined to form an enclosure from which there was no escape. . . . Like cattle we had been herded into the corral, and the gate had been barred behind us.[4]

Other cities isolated their Jews behind stone walls, wooden fences, or brick barricades. In Krakow, the ghetto wall was made of gravestones uprooted from Jewish cemeteries.

The purposes of the ghettos, like the forced labor camps, were to exploit the labor of the captive Jews and to provide more opportunities for "natural death" to wipe out the Jewish menace. In the spring of 1940, Hitler's armies had thundered through Europe, conquering one country after another: Denmark, Norway, Belgium, the Netherlands, and France. The German war machine was powerful, but it needed to be replenished. Plants were set up in and near the ghettos that would manufacture weapons and clothing for the German soldiers. When Hitler attacked the Soviet Union in June 1941, completely disregarding his promise to his ally Stalin, the need for labor became even more critical. So in the ghetto, Jewish people assembled uniforms for their captors and manufactured bullets for their enemy's guns.

Life in the Ghettos

Work was essential for the ghetto Jews. It gave them a sense of worth and dignity. It gave them something constructive to fill their dreary days and numbed minds. It permitted them to produce something of value they could exchange for food. But even with the demands for more and more arms, the Nazis did not have enough work to occupy all the Jews whose businesses and property they had stolen. All the forced labor camps and ghetto shops throughout the General Government probably never employed more than one fifth of the eligible labor force.[5]

Life in the ghetto was a daily struggle for work. Gone was the advantage of being a banker, lawyer, or stockbroker. For those not "employed" in the German ghetto industries and labor battalions, the only type of work that mattered was the production of merchandise that could be traded for food. Residents, deprived of their offices and shops, brought with them their sewing machines, cobbler's hammers, and other tools of their trades. Behind the stone walls they produced furniture, hats, and electronic equipment. Basements and attics of houses concealed mills that ground smuggled grain into flour. Handmade woolen socks and cotton gloves could be sold outside the ghetto for a few extra pieces of bread. Accountants' books from companies no longer in existence were taken apart, pressed together, and recast as cardboard briefcases. Hair brushes were made from goose feathers. Old sheets were dyed, cut, and transformed into scarves and handkerchiefs. Metal scraps became pots and pans. The resourcefulness of imprisoned residents—and the greed of their guards and of the Aryans and Poles beyond their fences—provided many of the ghetto Jews with the financial resources to buy just enough food to stay alive one more day.

For most, however, food was difficult to obtain. The German guards, of course, controlled everything coming into the ghetto. They sold bread and potatoes and a tiny bit of fat—nothing else—to the *Judenrat*, which, in turn, sold it to the people. At first the average ration amounted to about eleven hundred calories a day, but by the end of 1941 it had been reduced to eight hundred calories a day, which was half of what was allowed other Polish citizens.

More often than not, Jews in the ghetto received less than their ration cards permitted, and frequently the food was bad: stale, frozen, or spoiled. Sometimes potatoes that were too rotten to send to soldiers at the front were shipped to the ghettos. Sometimes the amount of food was so small that many of the ration coupons bought nothing more than potato peelings. For the first few months, some ghetto residents formed relief societies and ladled thin soup to long lines of hungry people. The soup kitchens were financed by aid from American organizations, which the Nazis permitted in hopes the United States would stay out of the war and because they kept some of the money. By the end of 1940, that scant supply line ran dry.

The residents turned to their own resources. In the tiny splotches of ground between buildings they planted radishes, onions, carrots, and turnips. They made soup from hay. They added chalk and powder to flour to stretch it among more people. They killed their horses and ate the meat. When that was gone, they mixed the horses' blood with salt and pepper and spread it on bread,[6] a practice forbidden by Jewish religious law but a necessary means of survival in the ghettos.

They smuggled life-giving food from the outside. Men employed in labor brigades exchanged clothing and personal items with Poles for bread or vegetables. Cart drivers slipped cow carcasses and sacks of grain into the ghetto in the empty wagons that had just carried their dead to cemeteries on the outside. Poles who lived in houses with doors on the "Aryan side" and windows on the ghetto side sometimes sold milk and cereal to the Jews. In utter defiance of the German authorities and at risk of certain death, courageous and desperate Jews made daily trips outside their prison. They scaled the nine-foot walls, dug under the fences, crawled through sewers, and squeezed through cracks in the stone. The youngest boys were often the best smugglers, but the Nazi guards showed no mercy when small children were caught. They executed them with no more pity or ceremony than they gunned down anyone else who dared oppose them.

Life in the ghetto was a daily struggle for health. By purposeful design, the houses were horribly overcrowded. A doctor in the Vilna ghetto reported that the twenty five thousand people there lived "in 72 buildings on 5 street sections. Comes to 1 1/2-2 meters per person, narrow as the grave."[7] There was not enough soap or water, and not enough toilets. Sewer pipes froze, and the contents of unusable toilets were dumped in the streets along with the garbage. When new refugees were brought into the ghetto, any disease they brought with them swept through the weakened, dirty residents with deadly speed.

Fighting the epidemics was nearly impossible. A nurse described the conditions in the Warsaw "hospital":

> It is a real hell. Children sick with the measles, two or three in one bed. . . . Shaven heads covered with sores swarming with lice. . . . No linens, no covers, no bedclothes. . . . There is no coal. The rooms are terribly cold. They huddle under the covers, shaking with fever.[8]

Typhus was the most common plague, but other maladies claimed even more lives. In the Lodz ghetto, heart disease, dysentery, and tuberculosis killed men, women, and children every day. In Warsaw, forty-three thousand people died in 1941 from the twin ravages of hunger and disease. One hundred to two hundred burials took place every day.[9]

Eventually there was no more space or strength left to dig graves. The dead were hidden as long as possible so the living could purchase extra food with their ration cards. Then their bodies were tossed in the streets with

In April of 1943, Jews in the Warsaw ghetto of Poland staged an uprising against their Nazi oppressors. The Germans crushed the uprising and killed many Jews to avenge the insurrection.

others—naked and uncovered, so the not-yet-dead could warm themselves with the clothes from those who needed them no longer. Emanuel Ringelblum, who chronicled the life and death of the Warsaw ghetto, observed that there came a point when "the sight of people falling dead in the middle of the street no longer stirred people." Children were not afraid of corpses, and adults were not saddened at the sight of frozen children.[10]

Life in the ghetto was a daily struggle to maintain hope. Even with the hourly preoccupation with survival, the Jews of Poland fed their souls. They organized lectures, concerts, and theater performances.

They formed lending libraries and reading circles with the books they could find, and they studied the works of great authors. They educated their children and adults in forbidden schools, wrote stories, and kept diaries. They recited their prayers, celebrated all their religious holidays, and took comfort in their holy books.

But rumors filtered into the enclosed ghettos in 1942, rumors too monstrous to be believed. In the east, on the border between Poland and the Soviet Union, the final stage of the Holocaust had begun.

Extermination
(1942–1945)

6

The concept of a Final Solution—a total and lasting end—to the "Jewish Problem" had been discussed in Germany for some time. Hitler had made his personal desire to "wipe out" the Jews clear in *Mein Kampf* long before he came to a position of power. Prior to the German invasion of Poland, Hitler warned that if a second world war should begin, "the result will be . . . the annihilation of the Jewish race throughout Europe." Five different times, in public addresses, he repeated his prophecy almost word for word: "The outcome of this war will be the extermination of Jewry."[1]

On June 30, 1934, just five months after being named chancellor, Hitler had orchestrated more than one hundred deaths, including that of Ernst Röhm— his friend of fourteen years, who had stood beside him at the Beer Hall Putsch and had commanded the Storm Troops.[2] At about the same time he launched the war, Hitler issued an order to kill German citizens who

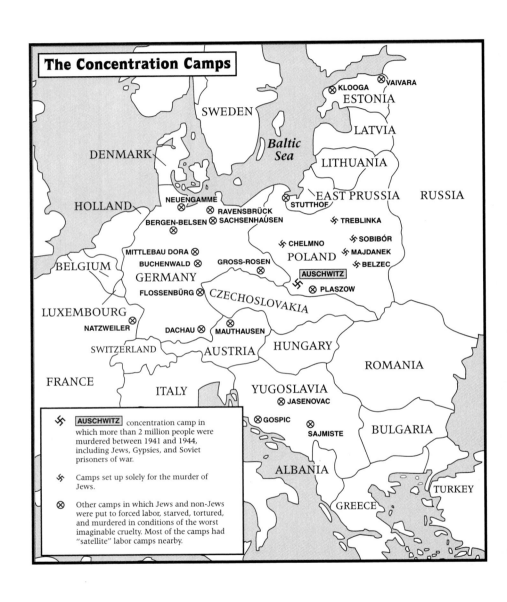

The Concentration Camps

VAIVARA
KLOOGA
ESTONIA

SWEDEN

LATVIA

Baltic
Sea

DENMARK

LITHUANIA

EAST PRUSSIA   RUSSIA

HOLLAND

NEUENGAMME
STUTTHOF
RAVENSBRÜCK
BERGEN-BELSEN SACHSENHAUSEN
TREBLINKA

BELGIUM

MITTLEBAU DORA
BUCHENWALD GROSS-ROSEN
GERMANY
FLOSSENBÜRG CZECHOSLOVAKIA

CHELMNO
POLAND
AUSCHWITZ
PLASZOW

SOBIBÓR
MAJDANEK
BELZEC

LUXEMBOURG
NATZWEILER   DACHAU MAUTHAUSEN
SWITZERLAND AUSTRIA HUNGARY

ROMANIA

FRANCE
ITALY   YUGOSLAVIA
JASENOVAC

GOSPIC
SAJMISTE
BULGARIA

ALBANIA

TURKEY

GREECE

AUSCHWITZ concentration camp in which more than 2 million people were murdered between 1941 and 1944, including Jews, Gypsies, and Soviet prisoners of war.

Camps set up solely for the murder of Jews.

Other camps in which Jews and non-Jews were put to forced labor, starved, tortured, and murdered in conditions of the worst imaginable cruelty. Most of the camps had "satellite" labor camps nearby.

were in mental institutions, who had physical defects, or who were incurably ill to relieve their suffering and to relieve Germany of the financial burden of caring for them. By August 1941, more than fifty thousand "mercy killings" had been carried out.

No one could doubt Hitler's capability for mass murder. Nor could anyone doubt the ability and willingness of his men to participate in genocide. They had demonstrated their ruthless disregard for Jewish lives and feelings in hundreds of street riots and arrests. They had shown their eagerness for violence on Kristallnacht. They had proven themselves capable of taking the lives of old people and young children in the cities of Poland. The Nazis were well able to execute a program of cold-blooded killing.

The fact that the Final Solution was ethnic murder does not appear in any official, written document of the Third Reich. Yet all the political and SS leaders seemed to be aware that a solution to the Jewish problem was planned and that it would, indeed, be final. Reinhard Heydrich, as head of the Central Emigration Office for Jews, claimed in a letter dated November 6, 1941, that he had "been entrusted for years with the task of preparing the final solution of the Jewish problem."[3] When he wrote to his *Einsatzgruppen* commanders in Poland in September 1939 of the "ultimate aim," he was careful to keep from putting on paper any explanation of what that aim was. He warned them that the

This map shows the locations of the largest concentration and death camps set up throughout the Nazi controlled regions of Europe. Hundreds of smaller, often temporary, camps completed the network. Special attention is given to Auschwitz, the most infamous of the camps.

"planned overall measures" were to be kept "strictly secret."[4]

Even before annihilation became the unwritten but official policy of the Nazi regime, all the German officials in the General Government in Poland seemed to understand that the ultimate purpose of the labor camps and the ghettos was to speed up the "natural deaths" of the Jews. Governor Frank justified his reduction in rations for the Jews of the Warsaw ghetto in October 1941 with this explanation: "During the winter the death rate will doubtless go up, but this war involves the total annihilation of Jewry."[5]

It was the war, more than anything else, that permitted the last stage of the Holocaust to take place. The war gave Hitler vast tracts of land where he could carry out his murderous program far from any critical eye. The war brought hundreds of thousands of Jews under Hitler's domination. The war provided a "cover" that lent a false justification to fiendish acts of cruelty. The act of war that triggered the start of the final phase of the Holocaust was the German invasion of the Soviet Union.

Dubbed Operation Barbarossa after a twelfth-century emperor, the campaign to "bring Russia to her knees" was scheduled to begin with lightning surprise in the early morning of June 22, 1941, and be over before winter. Within the first two weeks, ninety Soviet divisions had been defeated and one hundred fifty thousand soldiers taken prisoner. Half the Soviet Air Force was in pieces and thousands of Soviet tanks and guns were in German hands. The German Army advanced deep inside the Soviet Union.

Wannsee Conference

Cheered by the certainty of an early victory, Hermann Göring, Hitler's second-in-command, sent Reinhard Heydrich a directive on July 31, 1941. The order came

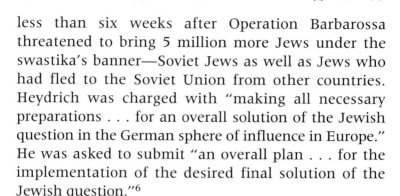

less than six weeks after Operation Barbarossa threatened to bring 5 million more Jews under the swastika's banner—Soviet Jews as well as Jews who had fled to the Soviet Union from other countries. Heydrich was charged with "making all necessary preparations . . . for an overall solution of the Jewish question in the German sphere of influence in Europe." He was asked to submit "an overall plan . . . for the implementation of the desired final solution of the Jewish question."[6]

Heydrich had already set the Final Solution in motion, but he called together representatives of all the departments that dealt with the Jewish problem. They met on January 20, 1942, in Wannsee, outside Berlin. Five SS officers attended together with nine government ministers.

As with all previous discussions of a total end to the Jewish question, very little was committed to paper. The few sentences that were recorded in the minutes spelled out the solution indirectly, but the meaning was still clear: All Jews would be exterminated. Jews scattered throughout Europe would be brought to the east—to eastern Poland or the soon-to-be-conquered Soviet Union—and they would be forced to work until they died of exhaustion, starvation, or exposure. Any who survived the rigorous labor would simply be executed.

The Wannsee Conference gave official sanction to a policy that was already in operation. The thinly disguised, deliberate attempt to exterminate Jews had actually begun months earlier, during the planning for Operation Barbarossa. It had started with the transformation of the *Einsatzgruppen* into mobile killing squads.

The *Einsatzgruppen*

The mobile SS detachments were not killing squads before the invasion of the Soviet Union. In Austria,

Czechoslovakia, and Poland, the task of these units was to arrest the political enemies of Germany and place them in concentration camps. But from the start of the Soviet campaign, all restraints were off. Hitler had told the chiefs of his armed services that the war against the Soviet Union was to be conducted "with unprecedented, merciless and unrelenting harshness."[7] He demanded that all his soldiers ignore any international law that would keep them from completely liquidating their enemy. So the *Einsatzgruppen*'s thirst for blood was given free rein.

In May 1941, while the German Army waited impatiently on the borders of the Soviet Union, Heydrich gave his *Einsatzgruppen* troops their orders. They were to follow the army and mop up after it. The military would eliminate all Soviet soldiers in its path through the country; the SS men would take care of the civilians. In every city and village the army conquered, the *Einsatzgruppen* was to ferret out "hostile inhabitants" and kill them. They were to execute Soviet commissars (leaders), the handicapped, gypsies, and Jews.

To accomplish this task, Heydrich divided his forces into four groups of five hundred to nine hundred each. Group A was sent to the Baltic States in the north: Estonia, Latvia, and Lithuania. Group B was assigned the central area known as Belorussia or White Russia. The Ukraine was the responsibility of Group C, and the area around the Black Sea was entrusted to Group D. Immediately after Operation Barbarossa began, the *Einsatzgruppen* sprang into action. Seven months before the Wannsee Conference, before extermination became the official policy, the final phase of the Holocaust was under way.

The weapons used by the mobile killing squads were primarily pistols, rifles, and submachine guns. The tactics were deception and force. When they entered a town, they usually found a respected rabbi and ordered him to gather together all the Jews. They were going to be "resettled," the Nazis said, "in another place."

When the Jews were assembled, they were marched out of town to the edge of a giant pit. Sometimes the gaping holes were antitank ditches dug in vain by the retreating Soviet army. Other times the victims had to dig their own trenches. Men, women, and children were lined up at the rim of the pit, sometimes on their feet and sometimes on their knees, and shot in the back of the neck. Many times victims were ordered to lie in the ditch, on top of their comrades, so they could be killed more easily. The dirt that filled the mass graves muffled the cries of anyone who survived the gunshot.

In the first few weeks, the German Army advanced rapidly and the *Einsatzgruppen* had to move quickly to the next location, before their prey escaped. All Jews they could not execute within a few days were locked into prisons or ghettos to await a second sweep of the killing squads.

The extermination of 2 million Jews in Soviet-held territory and another 3 million in Russia proper was a massive undertaking. The SS units enlisted the help of local people. In much of the Soviet Union, especially in Lithuania and the Ukraine, anti-Semitic feeling was strong. The Nazi executioners welcomed the participation of Soviet citizens. It allowed them to shift or at least share blame and to speed up their work. In the first five months of Operation Barbarossa, the *Einsatzgruppen* massacred half a million Jewish civilians. Then, they went back to liquidate the ghettos they had hastily established.

The largest single massacre recorded by these groups took place outside the Ukrainian city of Kiev.

As the atrocities against Jews heightened, mass executions became more common. Here, hundreds of Jewish men, women, and children have been forced into a ravine and await execution at the hands of the Nazis.

A land mine, left by the Soviet Army in its retreat, exploded in the city, destroying the hotel the German Army had taken for its headquarters. Hundreds of German soldiers were killed in the blast and the fires it ignited. SS officer Paul Blobel, one of the commanders of *Einsatzgruppe* C, blamed the Jews and took vengeance on them. He gave all the Jewish residents of Kiev three days to report for "resettlement." All those who responded, thinking they were being taken to a better, safer place, were marched in small groups to the edge of the Babi Yar ravine. A single shot in the back of the neck sent each one tumbling over the brink into the massive grave below. In two days (September 29 and 30, 1941), 33,771 Jews were killed at Babi Yar.

The men who formed the *Einsatzgruppen* were not soldiers, but policemen. Still, they were not unaccustomed to killing. During the many riots in Germany and the expulsions in the occupied territories, their brutality had been responsible for countless deaths. And they had long been conditioned to believe that Jews were subhuman creatures unworthy of life. But the deliberate, cold-blooded murder of waiting lines of people, one at a time, thousands per day, for weeks without end was almost too difficult for all but the most callous among them. Most of the squads were able to function only because the men were given great amounts of alcohol. One *Einsatzgruppen* leader, who admitted to killing ninety thousand Jews in a single year, confessed that the executions were a "moral strain" for his men. He insisted on using firing squads, never permitting only one person to shoot at a time, so that no one felt "direct personal responsibility" for taking the life of another. That, he said, would be "an immense burden to bear."[8]

Many of the officers, who preferred to leave the pulling of the triggers to the men under them, participated in the executions only as witnesses. They watched so they would not be accused of cowardice. One observer reported that Himmler himself—the man who had built the SS, who controlled all the police of the Reich, who was in charge of all concentration camps and labor camps—grew pale when faced with the work of the killing squads. Early in the program, Himmler had insisted on seeing the *Einsatzgruppen* in action. He attended a small execution: one hundred inmates of a prison in the town of Minsk. At the first crack of the weapons and the responses of the victims,

Himmler jolted, the color drained from his face, and he nearly fell to the ground.[9]

So for both the men who gave the orders and the ones who carried them out, explanations had to be devised that would ease their consciences. The killings were necessary, according to the official explanations, because the Jews had committed acts of sabotage. They had attacked German soldiers, bombed buildings, and started fires. Murder was justified because Jews were a threat to the occupation army. They spread disease. They spied for the enemy. They planned to attack Germany. Why must the children be killed, too? Because they would grow up to pose the same threat as their parents.

Even the Nazi language was carefully crafted to remove any sense of guilt. In the meticulous daily reports of the *Einsatzgruppen*, no one was ever killed. They were "resettled," "eliminated," or "liquidated." No slaughter ever took place. There were "actions," "special treatments," "executive measures," or "cleansings."

Whatever the words, when the *Einsatzgruppen* finished their work, more than one million Jews in the occupied Soviet Union were dead.

The mobile killing squads were obviously successful, but their methods were too slow for the Nazi high command and too messy. Himmler, shaken by his experience as a witness to an "action," asked Dr. Ernst Grawitz, the chief SS physician, what would be the most effective and efficient way of eliminating large numbers of people. The doctor recommended gas chambers.[10]

Gas Chambers

Poison gas was already being used to kill people in Germany. Just before the invasion of Poland that began World War II, Hitler had signed a secret order that

The Nazis sought quicker, more efficient means of extermination. The gas chamber was one method used in death camps to eliminate larger numbers of Jews and other prisoners. The furnace to the right created carbon monoxide for gassing prisoners.

allowed doctors "to grant a mercy death" to any of their patients who were not expected to get better. Six euthanasia (mercy killing) centers were set up for this purpose in hidden parts of the country. In these centers, ninety thousand people who were incurably sick, physically handicapped, mentally ill, or simply old were "humanely" murdered. In experimenting with different methods of killing these people, an SS officer, Christian Wirth, developed the gas chamber.

The gas chamber was an ideal instrument for large-scale murder. It was relatively quick and clean. It made no sound that would prematurely alert victims to their fate. A few men could dispense with many people at once. So gas chambers were installed in all six euthanasia institutes. Crematoriums were also built for each center to dispose of those who were killed by burning the bodies.

Once poison gas was found to be an effective agent of mass death, the architects of the Final Solution began to use it on Jews, even before the Wannsee Conference made extermination the official policy. They established six annihilation camps, all in Poland. These camps took over where the *Einsatzgruppen* left off. Their function was to eliminate the Jews of the ghettos of Poland and the Soviet Union. The liquidation of the ghettos and work camps of Poland in 1942 and 1943 became known as Operation Reinhard after Reinhard Heydrich was assassinated in May 1942. Use of the code name made it appear that the murders were committed in retaliation for Heydrich's death, but the extermination of Poland's Jews had been ordered four months earlier, at the Wannsee Conference.

Extermination Camps

The first Operation Reinhard camp, outside the small Polish village of Chelmno, began operation on December 8, 1941. It had no gas chamber but used five huge vans. Its victims were told they were going to be taken to Germany, where they would find work. First, however, they needed to shower and put on clean clothes. They undressed and walked happily to the washroom with the soap and towel they were given. When ninety unsuspecting people packed into the "washroom" that was really a van, the door was closed and the engine's exhaust was channeled into the crowded compartment. As the driver headed into the thick forest surrounding the camp, he listened for the screaming to stop. Then he drove deeper into the woods to a large, open pit. Jewish prisoners then opened the van and stacked the bodies of their friends and loved ones in a common grave and cleaned the truck for its next load.

When the warm weather came, the repulsive smell from the rotting corpses began to spread to nearby homes. The SS then built crematoriums and burned the remains of their new victims and of the thousands buried in the forest.

The primary purpose of Chelmno was to liquidate the 152,000 to 310,000 Jews in and around the ghetto of Lodz. That goal was achieved within fifteen months.

After the success of Chelmno, five more death camps were built, all in the General Government of Poland and all with stationary gas chambers rather than vehicles. The second camp, Belzec, was located just off the main railroad line that connected the ghettos of Lublin and Lvov and the concentration camp of Janowski. In its eight months of operation, six hundred thousand Jews were slaughtered—an average of twenty-five hundred per day.

Like Belzec, the Sobibor death camp was situated near the ghettos of the Lublin area of eastern Poland. An uprising among the Jews who were kept alive to do the grisly work of exploiting and disposing of the bodies shut the camp down after seventeen months. In total, an estimated two hundred fifty thousand perished at Sobibor.

The fourth extermination camp, Treblinka, was built specifically to eliminate the Warsaw ghetto and surrounding villages and towns. Because the gas chambers were not ready when the first "resettlement" trains came from Warsaw, the early victims were merely shot as they poured from the stifling train cars. Eventually the gas chambers were working so well that in the thirteen months before Treblinka was dismantled, eight hundred thousand were killed there.

The last two killing centers began a year or two earlier as concentration camps: Majdanek in July 1941 and Auschwitz in June 1940. The concentration camps were not designed to be the death chambers for Jews they eventually became. They were first built to detain the political enemies of Hitler. Communists, socialists, and others who disagreed with the Führer were tortured in these camps until they were no longer strong enough or brave enough to be a threat to the Nazi government. After the invasion of Poland, the camps took in prisoners of war from every country the Germans overran. Then, as the Soviet campaign bogged down in the bitter Soviet winter and waging war became harder and more costly, the camps were again transformed, this time into labor camps. The prisoners were forced to manufacture arms for their conquerors. In the hundreds of camps scattered throughout the Reich and the territories it held, inmates died daily—by design—of starvation, exposure to the elements, disease, overwork, and the brutality of the guards. Now, when the Final Solution of the Jewish problem became as important as winning the war, two of those labor camps added to their function the extermination of Jews.

At Majdanek, just over a mile from the city of Lublin, gas chambers were installed in late 1942. Of the 120,000 to 200,000 who died at Majdanek, fewer than half perished in the gas chambers. Many more succumbed to "natural causes" in the labor camp. Murder by machine gun was almost as common as by gas. In the single largest massacre in any camp, at least seventeen thousand Jewish inmates were shot to death in a planned rampage of hate on November 3, 1943.

The most notorious of the death camps was Auschwitz. By the time two farmhouses on the massive camp compound were equipped with gas chambers in July 1942, the labor camp was already a death factory. Prisoners were slain at a nearby euthanasia institute, inside the prison block, at the execution spot known as the "Wall of Death." But to accomplish the Final Solution, Auschwitz was greatly expanded by the construction of Auschwitz II (Birkenau). Four huge crematorium complexes were added, each with a gas chamber and five 3-door furnaces. Even these sixty ovens were not enough to dispose of the 1.25 million who perished there. Corpses were also burned in open pits.

Camp Operation

Once the ghettos of Poland and parts of the Soviet Union were liquidated, Jews were brought to

These Jews have arrived by train at Auschwitz where they await "selection." Some will be sent to the labor camp, but most will die in the gas chambers of Auschwitz.

Auschwitz and the other death camps from all over Europe. They came from the occupied lands of Holland, Belgium, France, Luxemburg, Denmark, Finland, Norway, Greece, and Yugoslavia. They came from the annexed countries of Austria and Czechoslovakia. They came from the allied nation of Italy and the cooperative countries of Hungary, Romania, and Bulgaria. And they came from Germany. In October 1942, Himmler ordered that all Jews in concentration camps in Germany be separated from other inmates and sent to Auschwitz.

They arrived by the thousands in cattle cars marked "worker resettlement." They filed quickly past an SS "doctor" for "selection"—some were motioned to the left, fit for work; most were sent to the right. Those on the right disrobed at the entrance to the "bath" and innocently entered the gas chambers. When they were dead, their fellow Jews, the ones who had been selected to live a week, a day, or an hour longer, stripped their bodies of everything that was of any value to their Nazi masters: rings, gold teeth, even hair. The lifeless remains were then burned in the crematoriums.

Furnaces eventually had to be installed in nearly all the concentration camps. For every camp, not only the six specifically designed as killing centers, became, after the Wannsee Conference, a part of the extermination program. Camp personnel were given not just the license, but the mandate, to work their Jewish

Women with small children and elderly women were automatically sent to the gas chambers (above). For these Hungarian women who were selected for work (bottom), their fate was slave labor.

prisoners—literally—to death. They had little difficulty carrying out their assignment.

The conditions in the camps were wretched enough in and of themselves to kill all but the hardiest. The unheated wooden barracks, with their row after row of three-, four-, or five-tiered platforms that served as beds, were miserably overcrowded, disgustingly filthy, and overseen by the most savage of the inmates. Rations of food were woefully inadequate and some camps had no water. Sanitation was almost nonexistent. In one camp, 120 people shared a single toilet.[11] Hunger and disease stalked every camp.

Many of the Jews who lived through the starvation and epidemics did not survive the rigors of heavy labor. They worked twelve-hour shifts in factories, farms, workshops, or stone quarries. If their pace was too slow for their slave masters, they were beaten or kicked until they either sped up or were completely unable to work. Some laborers at Dachau were forced to load crushed rocks into wagons so fast they fell beneath the whips of the guards.[12] Prisoners at Mauthausen who stumbled when pushing carts of stones up a mountainside were crushed by the weight of the wagons falling back on them.[13]

Those Jews who did not die of "natural causes" fell prey to the sadistic whims of the camp guards. At Mauthausen, probably the most brutal of all the camps, Jews were often pushed off the mountainside to the quarry floor, three hundred feet below. Others were chased into the camp's electrified wire fence and died of electrocution. Still others were forced outside the fence and ordered to run so the camp records could say "shot while trying to escape." At Janowski, prisoners returning from their twelve-hour workday were made to run through the camp to prove their physical fitness for the next day's labor detail. Those who dropped

These crematoria ovens in Buchenwald concentration camp were used to incinerate the remains of the dead. Fellow prisoners were forced to strip the corpses of anything useful to the Nazis and to prepare the bodies for cremation.

behind were taken outside the camp to the Valley of Death, also known as the Sands, and simply shot.[14]

Eventually the guards abandoned any attempt to justify or explain the murders. Some even killed Jews for sport, using them as targets for shooting contests.[15]

The causes of death were listed in the camp diaries, which were called the Death Books. The SS kept meticulous accounts of all that went on in certain camps. In others, the records were not well kept, and information about the prisoners was not considered as important. For the thorough camps, the number of prisoners in each transport, the countries from which they came, the amount of gold taken from the victims—all these figures were carefully recorded. For those whose labor could profit their tormentors before they died and for those who were selected for fiendish medical experiments, photographs were taken, numbers were tattooed on arms, and names were written in the ledgers. But in the annihilation camps, the nameless thousands who were driven directly from the railroad cars to the gas chambers were not entered into the Death Books.

Nowhere in the official records, however, do the Nazis admit to killing any of those who perished in the extermination camps. In both the written orders and the reports that followed, the "work" of these camps was referred to as "special treatment," "delousing," "disinfecting," "processing," or "special action." The vague vocabulary may have disguised the truth for a time, but it could not conceal it for long. The inoffensive words may have softened the sense of guilt for some of the executioners, but no words could remove the blood from their hands.

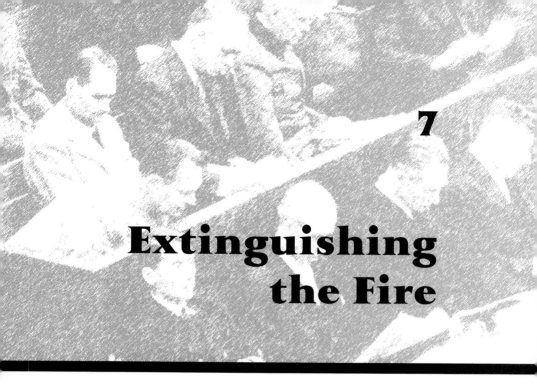

Extinguishing the Fire

The Holocaust ended short of its goal only because Germany lost the war. In the summer of 1944, German military defeat seemed certain. In the east, the Soviet Army had pushed Hitler's soldiers out of their country and stood ready to march into the Reich. In August, Soviet troops captured the oil fields of Romania that supplied nearly all the fuel for German tanks and trucks.

In the west, United States, British, and Canadian forces stormed the beaches of Normandy, France, on June 6, 1944. Within three months, 2 million Allied soldiers were sweeping across France toward Germany. Paris was liberated from Nazi control on August 25, 1944. Brussels, Belgium, was freed on September 3 and Antwerp, Belgium, on September 4.

Even when defeat was inevitable, the pace of the murder of Jews did not slacken. With the German Army in full retreat and in need of supplies and transportation,

When the concentration and death camps were liberated by allied forces, the stronger survivors would help their weak fellow prisoners reach the hospitals to receive medical attention. The world expressed outrage at the horrors uncovered in these camps as the true extent of the Holocaust began to be revealed toward the end of the war.

Adolf Eichmann was still given four trains per day in which to carry Jews to their deaths.[1]

Ending the Horror

The extermination sites were in danger of discovery. Chelmno and Belzec, the least efficient of the killing operations, had already been dismantled, and Treblinka and Sobibor had been destroyed after inmate revolts. Majdanek and Auschwitz, however, lay squarely in the path of the Soviet troops.

In a frantic attempt to kill as many Jews as possible before the Soviets reached the two camps, the SS ran the crematoriums round the clock. But the furnaces were not able to keep pace with the gas chambers and decaying bodies piled up. The guards worked feverishly to destroy all evidence of their grisly deeds: the Death Books, the canisters of gas, the rotting corpses, and the living witnesses. But the rapidly advancing soldiers did not give the Nazis time to kill all the Jews awaiting extermination.

As the Soviets drew close to Majdanek, the guards evacuated the Jewish inmates. They ordered the six thousand Polish prisoners who remained to burn the telltale signs of the camp's purpose. But the Poles, knowing that a shot in the back of the neck would be their reward, refused to destroy the incriminating evidence. Instead, they overpowered their captors and waited for liberation. The Soviet Army entered the camp on July 24, 1944, and the next day newspapers around the world shocked their readers with descriptions and pictures of human bones littered around five furnaces.

After Majdanek, all the concentration camps were subject to discovery and Germany to worldwide condemnation. With the Soviet Army moving quickly from the east and American and British forces closing in from the west, one camp after another was shut down to hide the terrible truth. The prisoners who could not be slain in time were evacuated—some in trains, most on foot—to camps in the narrowing strip of land that was still held by Germany.

The nearness of defeat did not soften the Nazis' attitude toward their prisoners. The forced march was simply another method of extermination. The weakened, emaciated victims were driven through rain and snow in nothing but their thin prison clothes. They marched for days, some for over a month. For many the journey covered more than four hundred miles. They had little, if any, food. Long columns of prisoners were kept moving by SS men on motorcycles with whips and guns and dogs. Any Jew who stopped to rest was shot. Anyone who fell out of formation was shot. Anyone who walked too slowly was shot. Rudolf Höss, a onetime commandant at Auschwitz, found the routes of the evacuees "easy to follow" because "every few hundred yards lay the bodies of prisoners who had collapsed or been shot."[2]

The death marches were the last gasps of Hitler's drive to completely destroy the Jewish people. He waged his campaign against the Jews until hours before his suicide and tried to continue it beyond his death. At 4:00 P.M. on the afternoon of April 29, 1945, the Führer of the Third Reich composed his Last Will and Testament. In it he accused the Jews of causing the war and blamed them for all the destruction the fighting had brought upon Germany. The final words the dictator left his nation the day before he ended his life called upon his followers to commit themselves to the misguided principle upon which he had based his reign: "Above all, I enjoin the government and the people to uphold the racial laws to the limit and to resist mercilessly the poisoner of all nations, international Jewry."[3]

But his men were no longer able to carry out their Führer's will. The soldiers of the Allies were quicker than the guns of the SS. The German Army surrendered,

This map indicates the estimated numbers of Jews killed during the Holocaust. The figures are broken down by country. As indicated, most victims came from Eastern Europe. Over 6 million Jews—11 million people altogether—were murdered during the Holocaust.

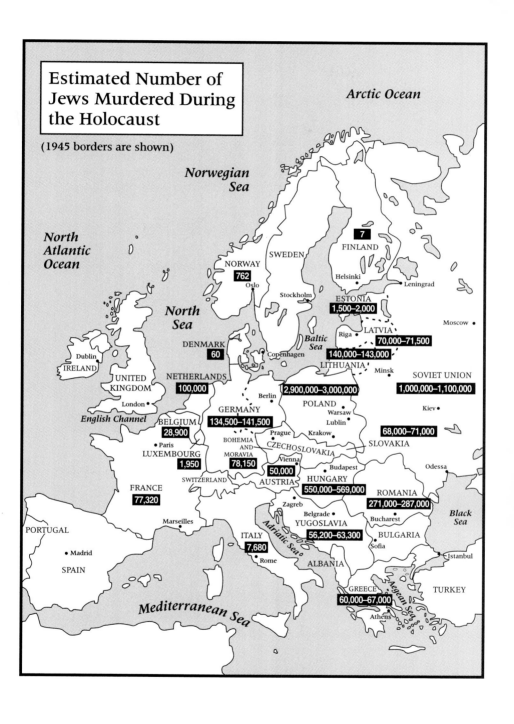

Estimated Number of Jews Murdered During the Holocaust

(1945 borders are shown)

Arctic Ocean

Norwegian Sea

North Atlantic Ocean

FINLAND
7

NORWAY
762
Oslo

SWEDEN

Helsinki

Leningrad

North Sea

Stockholm

ESTONIA
1,500–2,000

Baltic Sea

Moscow

DENMARK
60

Copenhagen

Riga

LATVIA
70,000–71,500

Dublin
IRELAND

NETHERLANDS
100,000

LITHUANIA
140,000–143,000

Minsk

SOVIET UNION
1,000,000–1,100,000

UNITED KINGDOM

London

Berlin

GERMANY
134,500–141,500

POLAND
Warsaw

Kiev

English Channel

BELGIUM
28,900

Paris

LUXEMBOURG
1,950

BOHEMIA AND MORAVIA
78,150

Prague

Krakow

Lublin

2,900,000–3,000,000

68,000–71,000

SLOVAKIA

CZECHOSLOVAKIA

Vienna

Budapest

Odessa

FRANCE
77,320

SWITZERLAND

AUSTRIA
50,000

HUNGARY
550,000–569,000

ROMANIA
271,000–287,000

Black Sea

Zagreb

Belgrade

Bucharest

Marseilles

YUGOSLAVIA
56,200–63,300

BULGARIA

Sofia

PORTUGAL

Madrid

ITALY
7,680

Rome

Adriatic Sea

ALBANIA

Istanbul

SPAIN

GREECE
60,000–67,000

Aegean Sea

TURKEY

Athens

Mediterranean Sea

camps and cities were liberated, and the war was over before the Final Solution could be completed. Three million of Europe's nine million Jews had survived.

Justice

A prophecy of one of Hitler's chief henchmen, Hermann Göring, also turned out to be wrong. At the very beginning of the Third Reich, in a speech delivered on March 3, 1933, Göring had predicted: "I don't have to worry about justice; my mission is only to destroy and exterminate, nothing more!"[4]

But in 1945 Göring did need to "worry about justice." For the entire world had been shaken and angered by the scenes of horror and the tales of atrocities that were crackling up from the ashes of the Third Reich. In country after country, Jews and non-Jews alike declared that crimes of such monstrous savagery cried out for punishment.

No precedent existed for punishing the types of deeds of which the Nazis were guilty. Representatives of the Allied governments struggled to define the offenses for which an international tribunal (court) could rightfully rebuke or condemn citizens of a sovereign nation. Two categories of unlawful acts were defined fairly easily: "crimes against peace" and "war crimes." These classifications covered all the brutality against soldiers and prisoners of war and against civilians in territories occupied as a result of war. But they

Hermann Göring was the commander of the German Luftwaffe during World War II. He earned a high position in the Nazi party and ordered Reinhard Heydrich to prepare a solution to the Jewish problem. Göring was put on trial at Nuremberg and was sentenced to death, but he committed suicide two hours before his execution was to be carried out.

did not extend to any mistreatment of civilians who resided in Germany. Nor was there any precedent for dealing with the attempt to murder an entire group of people. Finally, after fifteen attempts, the Allies defined a third type of offense:

CRIMES AGAINST HUMANITY: namely, murder, extermination, enslavement, deportation, and other inhumane acts committed against any civilian population, before or during the war, or persecutions on political, racial or religious grounds in execution of or in connection with any crime within the jurisdiction of the Tribunal, whether or not in violation of the domestic law of the country where perpetrated.[5]

The years following Germany's unconditional surrender on May 8, 1945, were marked by dozens of trials for crimes against humanity. The most important was conducted by a military court before judges from the United States, England, the Soviet Union, and France at Nuremberg, Germany. It opened November 20, 1945, with the reading of accusations against the twenty-two worst offenders the Allies were able to apprehend. The chief defendant was Hermann Göring.

Mountains of evidence were presented in the form of official documents, letters and diaries, photographs, and the testimony of eyewitnesses. A disbelieving world cringed as the revulsive revelations poured from the proceedings. When the trial ended after eleven grueling months, on the Jewish Day of Atonement, October 1, 1946, only three of the twenty-two had been found "not guilty." Four were sentenced to prison terms of ten, fifteen, and twenty years and three to life imprisonment. Twelve were condemned to death. However, Göring having finally been brought to the justice he had mocked twelve years earlier, bit into a smuggled capsule of poisonous cyanide and died in his cell two hours before he was to face the hangman's noose.

The highly publicized trial of the most prominent Nazi offenders by international tribunal was not the last. Twelve more cases were tried in Nuremberg before American military judges. They were trials of medical doctors; concentration camp officials; owners of companies that "employed" captive slave labor; and officers of the *Einsatzgruppen*. Of the 177 defendants, 117 were imprisoned and 25 sentenced to death.[6]

After the American proceedings, the British conducted several military tribunals. Smaller trials were held in the Netherlands, Denmark, Belgium, France, Czechoslovakia, Poland, Yugoslavia, and the Soviet Union. The Allied governments occupying Germany demanded that some war criminals be tried in German courts. As individual Nazis were captured, some even decades after the war ended, they were prosecuted by the countries that apprehended them. Many were executed for their part in the Holocaust. As of the printing of this book, more than fifty years after the Nuremberg tribunal defined crimes against humanity, the trials continue.

A holocaust is a sacrifice completely consumed by fire. The destruction of the Jews of Europe by the Nazis was fueled by a racism that had smoldered for centuries. The spark that ignited the flame was the appointment of Adolf Hitler as Chancellor of Germany. The bellows that fanned the blaze higher was the lightning-quick attack that launched World War II.

The fires of the Holocaust raged across nearly every country of Europe and consumed at least 11 million civilians: half a million gypsies; half a million French, Italian, and British civilians; 4 million Poles, Russians, Ukrainians, and other Slavs forced into slave labor; and 6 million Jews. About one million Jews perished as

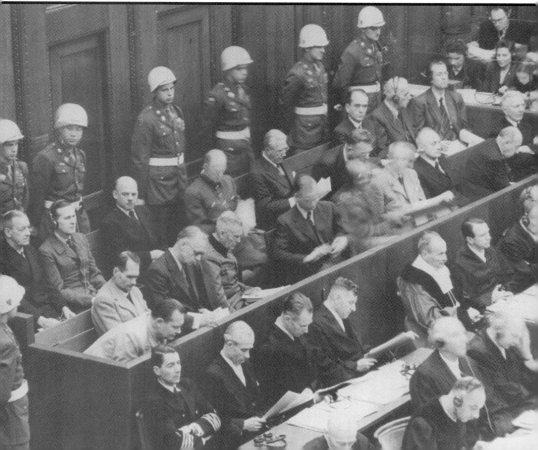

victims of the *Einsatzgruppen* and other firing squads. Two million died in the camps and ghettos from starvation, disease, overwork, or capricious cruelty. At least 3 million went to the furnaces of the death camps.

It took the armies of more than ten nations nearly six years to stop the Holocaust. It took decades of searches, arrests, and trials to extinguish the last, smoking embers. But the scars burned into the hearts and minds of the human race will never be completely healed. They remain as stark reminders of the human capacity for inhumanity. They testify to the danger of investing absolute power in the hands of any one person. They serve as evidence that ideas lead to action and twisted ideas can grow into ugly, heinous acts. The indelible scars of the Holocaust strengthen the resolve of many nations that an attempt at wholesale destruction of any people will never be tolerated again.

The world has fallen short of fully realizing the lessons of the Holocaust. Since the end of World War II, many peoples have suffered atrocities at the hands of others. In the shadow of the Holocaust, attempts at genocide still take place. This is why the story of the Holocaust must continue to be told. People everywhere must know the terrible reality that horrors like those of the Holocaust can happen again. The world must never forget.

Following the collapse of the Third Reich and the end of World War II, the surviving leaders of the Nazi party were put on trial as war criminals at Nuremberg. Most were found guilty of war crimes and crimes against humanity and were sentenced to death or long prison terms. In the bottom photograph, Hermann Göring can be seen leaning forward at the left. Rudolf Hess is seated to Göring's left.

Chronology

January 30, 1933
Hitler becomes chancellor of Germany.

February 27, 1933
Reichstag is set on fire.

February 28, 1933
Emergency decree "For the Protection of People and State" abolishes many constitutional guarantees of freedom.

March 22, 1933
Dachau, the first concentration camp, is opened.

March 23, 1933
Enabling Act is passed, giving Hitler absolute power.

April 1, 1933
Jewish businesses are boycotted throughout Germany.

September 15, 1935
First of the Nuremberg Laws is published, taking rights away from Jews.

March 13, 1938
Germany annexes Austria.

July 6–15, 1938
Evian Conference brings no solution to the problem of Jewish refugees.

October 28, 1938
First deportation order is issued, returning Polish Jews to Poland.

November 9–10, 1938
Kristallnacht: Nazi-instigated rampage against Jewish shops, known as Crystal Night or Night of Broken Glass.

March 15, 1939
Hitler occupies all of Czechoslovakia.

September 1, 1939
German invasion of Poland begins World War II.

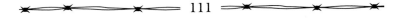

November 23, 1939
All Jews in Poland's General Government are required to wear Star of David.

April 30, 1940
First enclosed ghetto, in Lodz, Poland, is sealed.

November 15, 1940
Warsaw ghetto is sealed.

May 1941
Einsatzgruppen are readied for action in the Soviet Union.

June 22, 1941
Germany invades the Soviet Union.

September 28–29, 1941
Almost thirty-four thousand Jews from Kiev are massacred at Babi Yar.

December 8, 1941
First extermination camp is opened at Chelmno, Poland.

January 20, 1942
Wannsee Conference discusses final solution.

March 16, 1942
Extermination camp Belzec is opened in Poland.

May 1942
Extermination camp Sobibor is opened in Poland.

July 1942
Gas chambers are installed at Auschwitz.

July 23, 1942
Extermination camp Treblinka is opened in Poland.

Late 1942
Gas chambers are installed at Majdanek.

April 19–May 16, 1943
Warsaw ghetto is liquidated.

September–November, 1943
Ghettos in occupied Soviet Union are liquidated.

July 24, 1944
Soviets liberate Majdanek.

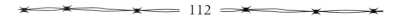

April 30, 1945

Hitler commits suicide.

May 8, 1945

Allies accept Germany's unconditional surrender.

November 20, 1945

War criminal trials begin at Nuremberg before an international tribunal.

Chapter Notes

Anti-Semitism

1. William L. Shirer, *The Rise and Fall of the Third Reich: A History of Nazi Germany* (New York: Simon & Schuster, 1960), pp. 233–234.

Chapter 1. Climate of Hate

1. Nora Levin, *The Holocaust: The Destruction of European Jewry, 1933–1945* (New York: Thomas Y. Crowell, 1968), p. 15.

2. Lucy S. Dawidowicz, *The War Against the Jews, 1933–1945* (New York: Holt, Rinehart and Winston, 1975), p. 45.

3. Ibid., p. 38.

4. William L. Shirer, *The Rise and Fall of the Third Reich: A History of Nazi Germany* (Greenwich, Conn.: Simon & Schuster, 1959), p. 96.

5. Ibid., p. 81.

6. Martin Gilbert, *The Holocaust: A History of the Jews of Europe During the Second World War* (New York: Holt, Rinehart and Winston, 1985), p. 21.

7. Leni Yahil, *The Holocaust: The Fate of European Jewry,* trans. Ina Friedman and Haya Galai (New York: Oxford University Press, 1990), p. 40.

8. The expression was first penned by Heinrich von Treitschke, a well-respected history professor at the University of Berlin, in 1879 in the *Preussische Jahrbücher.*

9. Dawidowicz, p. 46.

10. Gilbert, pp. 25–30.

11. Speech delivered by Hitler on October 13, 1920, entitled, "Why We Are Anti-Semites."

Chapter 2. Apostle of Violence

1. Konrad Heiden, *Der Fuehrer: Hitler's Rise to Power* (Boston: Houghton Mifflin, 1969), p. 190.

2. John Toland, *Adolf Hitler,* 2 vols. (Garden City, N.Y.: Doubleday, 1976), p. 109.

3. Speech delivered by Adolf Hitler in 1923.

4. Statement released by Adolf Hitler in 1937.

5. August Kubizek, *The Young Hitler I Knew* (Boston: Houghton Mifflin, 1954), p. 50.

6. William L. Shirer, *The Rise and Fall of the Third Reich: A History of Nazi Germany* (Greenwich, Conn.: Simon & Schuster, 1959), p. 33.

7. Kubizek, pp. 54–55.

8. Adolf Hitler, *Mein Kampf*, trans. Ralph Manheim (Boston: Houghton Mifflin, 1943), p. 21.

9. Ibid.

10. Hitler, p. 64. According to his friend, however, Hitler was firmly anti-Semitic before he came to Vienna (Kubizek, p. 79).

11. Hitler, p. 193.

12. Martin Gilbert, *The Holocaust: A History of the Jews of Europe During the Second World War* (New York: Holt, Rinehart and Winston, 1985), p. 24.

13. Werner Maser, ed., *Hitler's Letters and Notes* (New York: Bantam, 1976), p. 210.

14. Hitler, p. 30.

15. Hermann Rauschning, *The Voice of Destruction* (New York: G. P. Putnam's Sons, 1940), p. 83.

16. Hitler, p. 44.

17. Hitler, p. 497.

18. Kurt Ludecke, *I Knew Hitler: The Story of a Nazi Who Escaped the Blood Purge* (London: Scribner, 1938), pp. 217–218.

19. Shirer, pp. 170–171.

20. Shirer, p. 195.

21. Proclamation made to the Nazi Party Congress in Nuremberg, September 4, 1934, cited in Shirer, pp. 318–319.

22. Hitler, p. 65.

23. Gilbert, p. 31.

Chapter 3. Exclusion (1933–1938)

1. William L. Shirer, *The Rise and Fall of the Third Reich: A History of Nazi Germany* (Greenwich, Conn.: Simon & Schuster, 1959), p. 271.

2. Leni Yahil, *The Holocaust: The Fate of European Jewry*, trans. Ina Friedman and Haya Galai (New York: Oxford University Press, 1990), p. 60.

3. Barbara Distel and Ruth Jakusch, eds., *Concentration Camp Dachau 1933–1945* (Munich, Germany: Comité International de Dachau, 1978), p. 31.

4. Nazi newspaper, *Völkischer Beobachter*, March 31, 1933, in Nora Levin, *The Holocaust: The Destruction of European Jewry, 1933–1945* (New York: Thomas Y. Crowell, 1968), p. 43.

5. Robert Weltsch, "Wear the Yellow Badge with Pride," *Out of the Whirlwind: A Reader of Holocaust Literature*, ed. Albert H. Friedlander (Garden City, N.Y.: Doubleday, 1968).

6. Levin, p. 44.

7. Yahil, p. 76.

8. Levin, p. 75.

9. The official report said 815 shops were looted, but the number was later revised. See Gerald Reitlinger, *The Final Solution: The Attempt to Exterminate the Jews of Europe, 1939–1945*, 2nd rev. and aug. ed. (New York: Thomas Yoseloff, 1968), p. 16.

10. The official report said 36, but the report was admittedly an underestimate. The figure was later revised. See Yahil, p. 111.

Chapter 4. Expulsion (1938–1940)

1. Werner Maser, ed., *Hitler's Letters and Notes* (New York: Bantam, 1976), p. 210.

2. Leni Yahil, *The Holocaust: The Fate of European Jewry*, trans. Ina Friedman and Haya Galai (New York: Oxford University Press, 1990), p. 106.

3. Martin Gilbert, *The Holocaust: A History of the Jews of Europe During the Second World War* (New York: Holt, Rinehart and Winston, 1985), p. 64.

4. Nora Levin, *The Holocaust: The Destruction of European Jewry, 1933–1945* (New York: Thomas Y. Crowell, 1968), p. 78.

5. William L. Shirer, *The Rise and Fall of the Third Reich: A History of Nazi Germany* (New York: Simon & Schuster, 1960), p. 448.

6. Nora Levin, *The Holocaust: The Destruction of European Jewry, 1933–1945* (New York: Thomas Y. Crowell, 1968), p. 43.

7. Martin Gilbert, *The Holocaust: A History of the Jews of Europe During the Second World War* (New York: Holt, Rinehart and Winston, 1985), pp. 78–79.

8. Adolf Hitler, *Mein Kampf*, trans. James Murphy (London: Hurst and Blackett, 1939), p. 354.

9. Ibid., p. 84.

10. Shirer, pp. 259–260.

11. Gilbert, p. 84.

12. Arno J. Mayer, *Why Did the Heavens Not Darken? The "Final Solution" in History* (New York: Pantheon, 1988), p. 182.

13. Lucy S. Dawidowicz, *The War Against the Jews, 1933–1945* (New York: Holt, Rinehart and Winston, 1975), p. 116.

14. Gilbert, pp. 93–95.

15. Gerald Reitlinger, *The Final Solution: The Attempt to Exterminate the Jews of Europe, 1939–1945*, 2nd rev. and aug. ed. (New York: Thomas Yoseloff, 1968), p. 42.

16. Gilbert, p. 106.

Chapter 5. Enclosure (1940–1942)

1. Leni Yahil, *The Holocaust: The Fate of European Jewry*, trans. Ina Friedman and Haya Galai (New York: Oxford University Press, 1990), p. 157.

2. Yahil, p. 157.

3. Lucy S. Dawidowicz, *The War Against the Jews, 1933–1945* (New York: Holt, Rinehart and Winston, 1975), p. 202; Martin Gilbert, *The Macmillan Atlas of the Holocaust* (New York: Macmillan, 1982), p. 39.

4. Tosha Bialer, in Nora Levin, *The Holocaust: The Destruction of European Jewry, 1933–1945* (New York: Thomas Y. Crowell, 1968), p. 208.

5. *The Black Book* (New York: American Jewish Black Book Committee, 1945), p. 194.

6. David Wdowinski, *And We Are Not Saved* (New York: Philosophical Library, 1963), p. 42.

7. Dawidowicz, p. 208.

8. Levin, p. 222.

9. Wdowinski, p. 39.

10. Levin, p. 229.

Chapter 6. Extermination (1942–1945)

1. Speech delivered on January 30, 1942.

2. Reports of the number killed in the Röhm purge vary from Hitler's figure of 77 to other published estimates of 401 and more than 1,000. See William L. Shirer, *The Rise and Fall of the Third Reich: A History of Nazi Germany* (Greenwich, Conn.: Simon & Schuster, 1959), p. 310.

3. Gerald Reitlinger, *The Final Solution: The Attempt to Exterminate the Jews of Europe, 1939–1945*, 2nd rev. and aug. ed. (New York: Thomas Yoseloff, 1968), pp. 330–331.

4. Martin Gilbert, *The Holocaust: A History of the Jews of Europe During the Second World War* (New York: Holt, Rinehart, and Winston, 1985), pp. 88–89.

5. Reitlinger, pp. 56–57.

6. Nora Levin, *The Holocaust: The Destruction of European Jewry, 1933–1945* (New York: Thomas Y. Crowell, 1968), p. 290.

7. Shirer, p. 1,088.

8. Otto Ohlendorf, cited in numerous sources.

9. Reitlinger, pp. 221–222.

10. Raul Hilberg, *The Destruction of the European Jews* (Chicago: Quadrangle, 1961), p. 562.

11. Shirer, p. 1,238.

12. William W. Quinn (comp.), *Dachau* (unpublished reports compiled and distributed by the 7th U.S. Army), p. 31.

13. Leni Yahil, *The Holocaust: The Fate of European Jewry*, trans. Ina Friedman and Haya Galai (New York: Oxford University Press, 1990), p. 530.

14. Ibid.

15. Martin Gilbert, *The Macmillan Atlas of the Holocaust* (New York: Macmillan, 1982), p. 233; and Yahil, pp. 268–269.

Chapter 7. Extinguishing the Fire

1. Leni Yahil, *The Holocaust: The Fate of European Jewry*, trans. Ina Friedman and Haya Galai (New York: Oxford University Press, 1990), p. 511.

2. Rudolf Höss, *Commandant of Auschwitz: The Autobiography of Rudolf Höss* (London: World Publishing, 1961), p. 169.

3. H. E. Trevor-Roper, *The Last Days of Hitler* (London: Macmillan, 1947), p. 185.

4. William L. Shirer, *The Rise and Fall of the Third Reich: A History of Nazi Germany* (Greenwich, Conn.: Simon & Schuster, 1959), p. 272.

5. Raul Hilberg, *The Destruction of the European Jews* (Chicago: Quadrangle, 1961), p. 687.

6. Ibid., p. 696.

Glossary

Anti-Semitism: Prejudice against Jewish people.

Aryan: Originally, people speaking certain languages. The Nazis misused the term, using it to denote what they called a race of people of Teutonic (Germanic) background who were, typically, tall, blond, and blue-eyed.

Auschwitz: One of the largest extermination centers, consisting of a number of extermination and labor camps, located in Poland.

Babi Yar: A ravine on the outskirts of Kiev, in the Soviet Union, where the *Einsatzgruppen* massacred more than thirty-three thousand Jews on September 29–30, 1941.

Barbarossa: Code name for the German military campaign against Russia.

Blackshirt or Black Guard: A member or members of the *Schutzstaffel* (SS).

Brownshirt: A member of the *Sturmabteilung* (SA).

Chancellor: One of the two highest offices in Germany's Weimar Republic (the other being president).

Concentration Camp: Prison for political and religious opponents of the Nazi government of Germany also used for ethnic and racial "enemies."

***Einsatzgruppen* (Action Groups):** Mobile units of the police or SS that followed the German Army into conquered territories. At first, they arrested enemies of Germany, but after the German invasion of Russia, the *Einsatzgruppen* killed Jewish civilians and others by the thousands.

Euthanasia: The practice of deliberately killing a person who is suffering from an incurable condition. The Nazis used the term for the killing of physically and mentally handicapped and the aged.

Final Solution: Euphemism for the planned killing of all the Jews of Europe.

Führer (Leader): Hitler became Führer of the Nazi party and, as chancellor and president of Germany, adopted the title "The Führer."

General Government: German name for the part of occupied Poland that was not annexed as part of the Reich.

Gestapo: The *Geheime Staatspolizei*, the State Secret Police.

Ghetto: Sections of cities into which the Nazis forced all Jews. The areas were surrounded by barbed wire or walls, and no one was permitted to leave.

Gypsies: Nomadic peoples living in Europe who traveled in caravans and were persecuted by the Nazis.

Holocaust: The attempt by the Nazi government of Germany to completely destroy the Jews of Europe during World War II, from 1939 to 1945.

Judenfrei **(Jew-free):** Term that meant that all Jews had been removed from a particular geographic area by either deportation or extermination.

Judenrat: Council of Jewish elders established by Nazis in the ghettos to administer Nazi orders and policies among the Jewish inhabitants.

Judenrein **(cleansed of Jews):** Term used interchangeably with *Judenfrei*.

Labor Camp: Concentration camp in which prisoners were forced to perform labor for the Nazis.

Lebensraum **(Living Space):** Land in Poland and Russia that Hitler thought belonged to the German people by right of their supremacy.

Nazi: A member of, or pertaining to, the National Socialist German Worker's party, a political organization based on principles of extreme nationalism, militarization, racism, and totalitarianism.

Nuremberg Laws: Two laws, followed by thirteen supplementary decrees, that distinguished between Aryans and Jews and deprived non-Aryans of nearly every civil and legal right.

Nuremberg Trial: Trial of twenty-two of the most prominent Nazi leaders after World War II ended, in 1945 and 1946, by military judges of the United States, England, France, and the Soviet Union.

Operation Reinhard: Code name for the operation aimed at the extermination of the Jews in the General Government of Poland. Named in memory of Reinhard Heydrich, the chief planner of the Final Solution who was killed in 1942, it involved the establishment of death camps.

Reich: The government of Germany. "The Reich" is often used to refer to the country of Germany, especially under Hitler. **Third Reich:** The government of Germany under Adolf Hitler, 1933–1945.

Schutzstaffel **(Protection Squad) (SS):** Originally an elite group that served as Hitler's personal bodyguard, the SS became, under Himmler, a huge military-like organization that provided staff for camp guards, police units, and some fighting detachments.

Storm Troops: Men of the *Sturmabteilung* (SA).

Sturmabteilung **(SA):** Nazi private police force, also called Storm Troops and Brownshirts.

Swastika: Symbol used as the emblem of the Nazi party—a cross with the ends bent to the right.

Synagogue: A Jewish house of worship.

Wannsee Conference: Gathering of Nazi leaders outside Berlin on January 20, 1942, at which the details of implementing the Final Solution were decided.

Warthegau: The western portion of Poland that was annexed to Germany after the German invasion of Poland on September 1, 1939.

Weimar Republic: The democratic government of Germany between the end of World War I (1918) and Hitler's establishment of the Third Reich in 1933.

Further Reading

Adler, David A. *We Remember the Holocaust*. New York: Henry Holt, 1989.

Altshuler, David A. *Hitler's War against the Jews: A Young Reader's Version of "The War against the Jews, 1933–1945" by Lucy S. Dawidowicz*. New York: Behrman House, 1978.

Atkinson, Linda. *In Kindling Flame: The Story of Hannah Senesh, 1921–1944*. New York: Lothrop, Lee and Shepard Books, 1985.

Bar Oni, Bryna. *The Vapor*. Chicago: Visual Impact, 1978.

Berwick, Michael. *The Third Reich*. New York: Putnam, 1971.

Eisner, Jack. *The Survivor*. New York: William Morrow, 1980.

Finkelstein, Norman H. *Remember Not to Forget: A Memory of the Holocaust*. New York: Franklin Watts, 1985.

Fluek, Toby Knobel. *Memories of My Life in a Polish Village, 1930–1949*. New York: Knopf, 1990.

Friedman, Ina R. *Escape or Die: True Stories of Young People Who Survived the Holocaust*. Reading, Mass.: Addison-Wesley, 1982.

Koehn, Ilse. *Mischling, Second Degree*. New York: Greenwillow Books, 1977.

Kuper, Jack. *Child of the Holocaust*. New York: Doubleday, 1967.

Melzer, Milton. *Never to Forget: The Jews of the Holocaust*. New York: Harper and Row, 1976.

Patterson, Charles. *Antisemitism: The Road to the Holocaust and Beyond*. New York: Walker, 1989.

Procktor, Richard. *Nazi Germany: The Origins and Collapse of the Third Reich*. New York: Holt, Rinehart and Winston, 1970.

Rogasky, Barbara. *Smoke and Ashes: The Story of the Holocaust*. New York: Holiday House, 1988.

Rossel, Seymour. *The Holocaust*. New York: Franklin Watts, 1981.

Rubin, Arnold. *The Evil That Men Do: The Story of the Nazis*. New York: Julian Messner, 1977.

Shirer, William. *Rise and Fall of Adolf Hitler*. New York: Random House, 1984.

Ten Boom, Corrie. *The Hiding Place*. Old Tappan, N.J.: Revell, 1971.

Treseder, Terry Walton. *Hear O Israel: A Story of the Warsaw Ghetto*. New York: Atheneum, 1990.

Werstein, Irving. *The Uprising of the Warsaw Ghetto, November 1940–May 1943*. New York: Norton, 1968.

Wiesel, Elie. *Night*. New York: Noonday Press, 1988.

Index